NEW BRITISH FICTION

NEW BRITISH FICTION

Julian Barnes

Frederick M. Holmes

palgrave
macmillan

First published 2009 by
PALGRAVE MACMILLAN

Palgrave Macmillan in the UK is an imprint of Macmillan Publishers Limited,
registered in England, company number 785998, of Houndmills, Basingstoke,
Hampshire RG21 6XS.

Palgrave Macmillan in the US is a division of St Martin's Press LLC,
175 Fifth Avenue, New York, NY 10010.

Palgrave Macmillan is the global academic imprint of the above companies
and has companies and representatives throughout the world.

Palgrave® and Macmillan® are registered trademarks in the United States,
the United Kingdom, Europe and other countries.

ISBN-13: 978–1–4039–9692–3 hardback
ISBN-10: 1–4039–9692–X hardback
ISBN-13: 978–1–4039–9693–0 paperback
ISBN-10: 1–4039–9693–8 paperback

This book is printed on paper suitable for recycling and made from fully
managed and sustained forest sources. Logging, pulping and manufacturing
processes are expected to conform to the environmental regulations of the
country of origin.

A catalogue record for this book is available from the British Library.

A catalog record for this book is available from the Library of Congress.

10   9   8   7   6   5   4   3   2   1
18   17   16   15   14   13   12   11   10   09

CONTENTS

GENERAL EDITORS' PREFACE

This series highlights with its very title two crucial elements in the nature of contemporary British fiction, especially as a field for academic research and study. The first term indicates the originality and freshness of such writing expressed in a huge formal diversity. The second evokes the cultural identity of the authors included, who nevertheless represent through their diversity a challenge to any hegemonic or narrow view of Britishness. As regards the fiction, many of the writers featured in this series continue to draw from and adapt long traditions of cultural and aesthetic practice. Such aesthetic continuities contrast starkly with the conditions of knowledge at the end of the twentieth century and the beginning of the twenty-first, a period that has been characterised by an apprehension of radical presentness, a sense of unprecedented forms of experience and an obsession with new modes of self-awareness. This stage of the survival of the novel may perhaps be best remembered as a millennial and postmillennial moment, a time of fluctuating reading practices and of historical events whose impact is largely still unresolved. The new fiction of these times reflects a rapidly changing cultural and ideological reality, as well as a renewal of the commitment of both writers and readers to both the relevance and utility of narrative forms of knowledge.

Each volume in this series will serve as an introductory guide to an individual author chosen from a list of those whose work has proved to be of general interest to reviewers, academics, students and the general reading public. Each volume will offer information concerning the life, work and literary and cultural contexts appropriate to the chosen subject of each book; individual volumes will share the same overall structure with a largely common organization of materials. The result is intended to be suitable for both academic and general readers: putting accessibility at a premium, without compromising

an ambitious series of readings of today's most vitally interesting British novelists, interpreting their work, assessing their
influences and exploring their relationship to the times in which
they live.

Philip Tew and Rod Mengham

ACKNOWLEDGEMENTS

I am grateful to Philip Tew for inviting me to submit a proposal for this book. Kate Haines, Commissioning Editor at Palgrave Macmillan, Felicity Noble, her secretary, and Kitty van Boxel, Assistant Editor, have all been helpful in answering my queries. I also wish to thank the librarians who work in the Inter-Library Loan Office of Lakehead University's Paterson Library. Without their services, I would have been unable to write this book. I appreciate the support of my colleagues in the Department of English at Lakehead University. My greatest debt is to my wife, Patricia Jasen, who patiently supported my efforts on this project. Several years ago, she contemplated writing an article on *Flaubert's Parrot*. After I began working on Barnes, she passed along to me the notes that she had made at that time, as well as the photocopies of reviews of the novel. I profited from them when I came to write my section on *Flaubert's Parrot*.

PART I
Introduction

TIMELINE

1960 Harold Macmillan 'Winds of Change' speech, Cape Town, South Africa
John F. Kennedy elected as US President
Aged six, Kazuo Ishiguro arrives in Britain

1961 Adolf Eichmann on trial in Israel for role in Holocaust
Bay of Pigs: attempted invasion of Cuba
Berlin Wall constructed
Yuri Gagarin first person in Space
Silicon chip patented
Private Eye magazine begins publication
Muriel Spark, *The Prime of Miss Jean Brodie*
Jonathan Coe born

1962 Cuban Missile Crisis
Marilyn Monroe dies
Independence for Uganda; followed this decade by Kenya (1963), Northern Rhodesia (1964), Southern Rhodesia (1965), Barbados (1966)

1963 John F. Kennedy assassinated in Dallas
Martin Luther King Jr delivers 'I Have a Dream' speech
Profumo Affair

1964   Nelson Mandela sentenced to life imprisonment
Commercial pirate radio challenges BBC monopoly

1965   State funeral of Winston Churchill
US sends troops to Vietnam
A. L. Kennedy born in Dundee, Scotland

1966   Ian Brady and Myra Hindley sentenced to life imprisonment for Moors Murders
England beats West Germany 4–2 at Wembley to win Football World Cup
Star Trek series debut on NBC television
Jean Rhys, *The Wide Sargasso Sea*

1967   Six-Day War in the Middle East
World's first heart transplant
Abortion Act legalizes termination of pregnancy in UK
Sergeant Pepper's Lonely Hearts Club Band album released by The Beatles
Flann O'Brien, *The Third Policeman*

1968   Anti-Vietnam War protestors attempt to storm American Embassy in Grosvenor Square
Martin Luther King Jr assassinated
Robert F. Kennedy assassinated
Student protests and riots in France
Lord Chamberlain's role as censor of plays in the UK is abolished
Lindsay Anderson, *If . . .*

1969   Civil rights march in Northern Ireland attacked by Protestants
Apollo 11 lands on the Moon with Neil Armstrong's famous first steps
Rock concert at Woodstock
Yasser Arafat becomes leader of PLO
Booker Prize first awarded; winner P. H. Newby, *Something to Answer for*

Open University founded in the UK
John Fowles, *The French Lieutenant's Woman*

1970 Popular Front for the Liberation of Palestine (PFLP) hijacks five planes
Students activists and bystanders shot in anti-Vietnam War protest at Kent State University, Ohio, four killed, nine wounded
UK voting age reduced from 21 years to 18

1971 Decimal currency introduced in the UK
Internment without trial of terrorist suspects in Northern Ireland begins
India and Pakistan in conflict, after Bangladesh declares independence

1972 Miners' strike
Bloody Sunday in Londonderry, 14 protestors killed outright or fatally wounded by British troops
Aldershot barracks bomb initiates IRA campaign with seven dead
Britain enters Common Market
Massacre of Israeli athletes at Munich Olympics
Watergate scandal
Anthony Burgess, *A Clockwork Orange*
Samuel Beckett, *Not I*

1973 US troops leave Vietnam
Arab–Israeli 15-day Yom Kippur War
PM Edward Heath introduces three-day working week
Martin Amis, *The Rachel Papers*

1974 Miners' strike
IRA bombings in Guildford (five dead) and Birmingham (21 dead)

1975 Microsoft founded
Sex Discrimination Act

Zadie Smith born in North London
Malcolm Bradbury, *The History Man*

1976   Weak economy forces UK government loan from the International Monetary Fund (IMF)
Ian McEwan, *First Love, Last Rites*

1977   *Star Wars* released
UK unemployment tops 1,600,000
Nintendo begins to sell computer games
Sex Pistols 'Anarchy in the UK' tour

1978   Soviet troops occupy Afghanistan
First test-tube baby born in Oldham, England

1979   Iranian Revolution establishes Islamic theocracy
Margaret Thatcher becomes PM after Conservative election victory
USSR invades Afghanistan
Lord Mountbatten assassinated by the IRA

1980   Iran–Iraq War starts
Iranian Embassy siege in London
CND rally at Greenham Common airbase, England
IRA hunger strike at Belfast Maze Prison over political status for prisoners
Julian Barnes, *Metroland*
Julian Barnes (under pseudonym Dan Kavanagh), *Duffy*

1981   Prince Charles and Lady Diana marry in St Paul's Cathedral with 750 million worldwide television audience
Widespread urban riots in UK including in Brixton, Holloway, Toxteth, Handsworth, Moss Side
AIDS identified
First IBM personal computer
Alasdair Gray, *Lanark*
Salman Rushdie, *Midnight's Children*, which wins Booker Prize for Fiction

Julian Barnes, Somerset Maugham Award (for *Metroland*)
Julian Barnes (under pseudonym Dan Kavanagh), *Fiddle City*

1982 Mark Thatcher, PM's son, disappears for three days in Sahara during the Paris-Dakar rally
Falklands War with Argentina, costing the UK over £1.6 billion
Body of Roberto Calvi, chairman of Vatican-connected Banco Ambrosiano, found hanging beneath Blackfriars Bridge, London
Julian Barnes, *Before She Met Me*

1983 Klaus Barbie, Nazi war criminal, arrested in Bolivia
Beirut: US Embassy and barracks bombing, killing hundreds of members of multinational peacekeeping force, mostly US marines
US troops invade Grenada
Microsoft Word first released
Salman Rushdie, *Shame*, which wins Prix du Meilleur Livre Etranger (France)

1984 Miners' strike
HIV identified as cause of AIDS
IRA bomb at Conservative Party Conference in Brighton kills four British Telecom privatization shares sale
Thirty-eight deaths during clashes at Liverpool v. Juventus football match at Heysel Stadium, Brussels
Martin Amis, *Money: A Suicide Note*
Julian Barnes, *Flaubert's Parrot*
James Kelman, *Busconductor Hines*
Graham Swift, *Waterland*

1985 Famine in Ethiopia and Live Aid concert
Damage to ozone layer discovered
Mikhail Gorbachev becomes Soviet Premier and introduces *glasnost* (openness with the West) and *perestroika* (economic restructuring)
PC Blakelock murdered during riots on Broadwater Farm estate in Tottenham, London

My Beautiful Laundrette film released (dir. Stephen Frears, screenplay Hanif Kureishi)

Jeanette Winterson, *Oranges Are Not the Only Fruit*

Julian Barnes, Geoffrey Faber Memorial Prize (for *Flaubert's Parrot*)

Julian Barnes (under pseudonym Dan Kavanagh), *Putting the Boot In*

1986   Abolition of Greater London Council and other metropolitan county councils in England

Violence between police and protestors at Wapping, East London after Rupert Murdoch sacks 5000 print workers

Challenger shuttle explodes

Chernobyl nuclear accident

US bombs Libya

Peter Ackroyd, *Hawksmoor*

Julian Barnes, Prix Médicis (France) and E. M. Forster Award (USA) (for *Flaubert's Parrot*)

Julian Barnes, *Staring at the Sun*

1987   Capsizing of RORO ferry, *Herald of Free Enterprise*, off Zeebrugge kills 193 people

London Stock Exchange and market collapse on 'Black Monday'

Remembrance Sunday: eleven killed by Provisional IRA bomb in Enniskillen

Ian McEwan, *The Child in Time*, which wins Whitbread Novel Award

Jeanette Winterson, *The Passion*

Julian Barnes, Gutenberg Prize

Julian Barnes (under pseudonym Dan Kavanagh), *Going to the Dogs*

1988   US shoots down Iranian passenger flight

Pan Am flight 103 bombed over Lockerbie, 270 people killed

Soviet troop withdrawals from Afghanistan begin

Salman Rushdie, *The Satanic Verses*

Julian Barnes, Grinzane Cavour Prize (Italy)

1989 Fatwa issued against Rushdie by Iranian leadership (Khomeini)

Fall of Berlin Wall

Exxon Valdez oil disaster

Student protestors massacred in Tiananmen Square, Bejing

Hillsborough Stadium disaster in which 96 football fans die

Kazuo Ishiguro, *The Remains of the Day*, which wins Booker Prize for Fiction

Jeanette Winterson, *Sexing the Cherry*

Julian Barnes, *A History of the World in 10^1/$_2$ Chapters*

1990 London poll tax riots

Fall of Thatcher; John Major becomes Conservative PM

Nelson Mandela freed from jail

Jeanette Winterson adapts *Oranges* for BBC television film

A. S. Byatt, *Possession*

Hanif Kureishi, *The Buddha of Suburbia*, which wins Whitbread First Novel Prize

A. L. Kennedy, *Night Geometry and the Garscadden Trains*

1991 Soviet Union collapses

First Iraq War with 12-day Operation Desert Storm

Apartheid ended in South Africa

PM Major negotiates opt-out for Britain from European Monetary Union and rejects Social Chapter of Maastricht Treaty

Hypertext Markup Language (HTML) helps create the World Wide Web

Hanif Kureishi: screenplays for *Sammy and Rosie Get Laid* and *London Kills Me* Pat Barker, *Regeneration*

Julian Barnes, *Talking It Over*

1992 'Black Wednesday' stock market crisis when UK forced to exit European Exchange Rate Mechanism

Adam Thorpe, *Ulverton*

Julian Barnes, Prix Femina (France) (for *Talking It Over*)

Julian Barnes, *The Porcupine*

1993   Black teenager Stephen Lawrence murdered in Well Hall Road, London
With Downing Street Declaration, PM John Major and Taoiseach Albert Reynolds commit Britain and Ireland to joint Northern Ireland resolution
Film of Ishiguro's *The Remains of the Day*, starring Anthony Hopkins and Emma Thompson
Irvine Welsh, *Trainspotting*
Julian Barnes, Shakespeare Prize

1994   Tony Blair elected leader of Labour Party following death of John Smith
Channel Tunnel opens
Nelson Mandela elected President of South Africa
Provisional IRA and loyalist paramilitary cease-fire
Homosexual age of consent for men in the UK lowered to 18
Mike Newell (dir.), *Four Weddings and a Funeral*
Jonathan Coe, *What a Carve Up!*
James Kelman, *How Late It Was, How Late*, which wins Booker Prize for Fiction
Irvine Welsh, *The Acid House*

1995   Oklahoma City bombing
Srebrenica massacre during Bosnian War
Pat Barker, *The Ghost Road*
Nicholas Hytner (dir.), *The Madness of King George*
Hanif Kureishi, *The Black Album*
Julian Barnes, *Letters from London*

1996   Cases of Bovine Spongeiform Encephalitis (Mad Cow Disease) in the UK
Divorce of Charles and Diana
Breaching cease-fire, Provisional IRA bombs London's Canary Wharf and Central Manchester
Film of Irvine Welsh's *Trainspotting* (dir. Danny Boyle), starring Ewan McGregor and Robert Carlyle
Graham Swift, *Last Orders*, which wins Booker Prize
Julian Barnes, *Cross Channel*

1997 Tony Blair becomes Labour PM after landslide victory
Princess Diana dies in Paris car crash
Hong Kong returned to China by UK
Jim Crace, *Quarantine*
Jonathan Coe, *The House of Sleep*, which wins Prix Médicis Etranger (France)
Ian McEwan, *Enduring Love*
Iain Sinclair and Marc Atkins, *Lights Out for the Territory*

1998 Good Friday Agreement on Northern Ireland and Northern Ireland Assembly established
Twenty-eight people killed by splinter group Real IRA bombing in Omagh
Sonny Bono Act extends copyright to lifetime plus 70 years
BFI/Channel 4 film *Stella Does Tricks*, released (screenplay A. L. Kennedy)
Julian Barnes, *England, England*

1999 Euro currency adopted
Macpherson Inquiry into Stephen Lawrence murder accuses London's Metropolitan Police of institutional racism
NATO bombs Serbia over Kosovo crisis
Welsh Assembly and Scottish Parliament both open
Thirty-one passengers killed in Ladbroke Grove train disaster

2000 Anti-globalization protest and riots in London
Hauliers and farmers blockade oil refineries in fuel price protest in the UK
Kazuo Ishiguro, *When We Were Orphans*
Will Self, *How the Dead Live*
Zadie Smith, *White Teeth*
Julian Barnes, *Love, etc.*

2001 9/11 Al-Qaeda attacks on World Trade Center and Pentagon
Bombing and invasion of Afghanistan

Riots in Oldham, Leeds, Bradford, and Burnley, Northern England

Labour Party under Blair re-elected to government

Ian McEwan, *Atonement*

2002   Queen Mother dies aged 101

Rowan Williams named next Archbishop of Canterbury

Bali terrorist bomb kills 202 people and injures a further 209

Inquiry concludes English general practitioner Dr Harold Shipman killed around 215 patients

Zadie Smith's *White Teeth* adapted for Channel 4 television broadcast in autumn

Julian Barnes, *Something to Declare*

Julian Barnes, translates and edits Alphonse Daudet's *In the Land of Pain*

2003   Invasion of Iraq and fall of Saddam Hussein

Death of UK government scientist Dr David Kelly, and Hutton Inquiry

Worldwide threat of Severe Acute Respiratory Syndrome (SARS)

Julian Barnes, *The Pedant in the Kitchen*

2004   BBC Director General Greg Dyke steps down over Kelly affair

Bombings in Madrid kill 190 people and injure over 1700

Expansion of NATO to include seven ex-Warsaw Pact countries

European Union expands to 25 countries as eight ex-communist states join

Jonathan Coe, *Like a Fiery Elephant: The Story of B. S. Johnson*

Alan Hollinghurst, *The Line of Beauty*, which wins Booker Prize for Fiction

Andrea Levy, *Small Island*, which wins Orange Prize for Fiction

Julian Barnes, Commandeur de l'Ordre des Arts et des Lettres (France) and Austrian State Prize for European Literature
Julian Barnes, *The Lemon Table*

2005   UK ban on foxhunting with dogs comes into force
7/7 London suicide bombings on transport system kill 52 and injure over 700 commuters in morning rush hour
Hurricane Katrina kills at least 1836 people and floods devastate New Orleans
After four failed bombings are detected, Brazilian Jean Charles de Menezes is shot and killed by Metropolitan Police officers at Stockwell Underground Station
Ian McEwan, *Saturday*
Zadie Smith, *On Beauty*, which wins 2006 Orange Prize for Fiction
Julian Barnes, *Arthur & George*

2006   Jeanette Winterson awarded the OBE
Airline terror plot thwarted, causes major UK airline delays
Israel–Hezbollah war in Lebanon
Five prostitutes killed in Ipswich in a six-week period
Saddam Hussein executed by hanging in controversial circumstances

1

INTRODUCTION

Julian Barnes came to prominence in the 1980s as a cosmopolitan, intellectually and culturally sophisticated fictional experimenter. He has said that '[i]n order to write, you have to convince yourself that it's a new departure not only for you but for the entire history of the novel' (Stout 4). Especially in *Flaubert's Parrot* (1984), the Booker Prize–nominated book that won him renown, he violated the conventional boundaries between the novel and other discursive forms while staking a claim to the literature (particularly Flaubert's writing) and culture of France as his special area of expertise. Yet Barnes is also a quintessentially English author in the sense that his *oeuvre* reflects his upbringing and education in the 1950s and 1960s and his subsequent experiences as a professional writer based in London. He grew up as a middle-class suburbanite who first commuted to London to attend a prestigious school and then went on to read modern languages at Oxford University before working as a lexicographer, studying law, and writing for publications such as the *New Review*, the *New Statesman*, and the *Observer*. Influenced as much by the literary traditions of his own country as by French writing, Barnes is interested in exploring different models of English identity that have come under pressure during an era dominated by global capitalism and what Fredric Jameson calls its postmodernist cultural logic. Clearly appalled at the ways in which commodified, depthless images projected by electronic media now serve in post-industrial societies as a prime matrix for identity formation, Barnes's fiction nevertheless itself displays a self-reflexive, postmodernist scepticism regarding any truth claims, even those which potentially could anchor personal identity and counter the simulacra of cyber culture. He destabilizes versions of national identity derived from England's past by refusing to treat his own representations of history as foundational.

Although, as his American friend and fellow novelist Jay McInerney notes (Stout 6), Barnes usually cultivates a Flaubertian impersonality as a novelist, it was nevertheless evident from the first that the creator standing invisibly behind his fictional worlds is culturally refined, formidably intelligent, and commandingly articulate. His first novel, the somewhat autobiographical *Metroland*, displays a comfortable familiarity with the worlds of art and literature— especially French literature; it is easy to infer on the evidence of this book alone that Barnes, like his young protagonist and narrator, Christopher Lloyd, is a devotee of aesthetic experience. As Rudolf Freiburg observes, Barnes's work is self-consciously intertextual (44), and it is packed with specific allusions to earlier works of literature by a wide range of authors. His novels and stories are also full of references to paintings, musical compositions and performances, and other cultural artefacts. *Flaubert's Parrot* tracks the life of a great French novelist and in the process reveals an intimate knowledge of works by and about him. *A History of the World in 10½ Chapters* contains sophisticated art criticism of Theodore Géricault's painting 'Scene of a Shipwreck', which is reproduced in a glossy colour photograph. *Cross Channel* and *The Lemon Table* contain stories featuring composers of symphonic music [based, according to Vanessa Guignery (*Fiction* 120), on Frederick Delius and Jean Sibelius]. The narrator of another story in *The Lemon Table*, 'The Silence', is based on the novelist and playwright Ivan Turgenev (Guignery, *Fiction* 123), and several surrealist writers, including André Breton and Raymond Queneau, appear in *Cross Channel's* 'Experiment'. Barnes's treatment of the various art forms features subtleties of detail and reference that could only be written by a highbrow deeply immersed in the arts and educated about their histories.

Yet the implied author that Barnes creates in his narratives is not an effete cultural snob, who worships at the shrine of high art and stigmatizes all manifestations of popular, mass culture as worthless. The implied readers fashioned by his novels are a diverse, inclusive lot, not a cultural elite devoted to the Arnoldian idea of 'the best that has been thought and known in the world' (*Poetry and Criticism* 426). Barnes's novels do not aspire to the status of sanctified aesthetic icons. He has expressed dissatisfaction with the pigeonhole of 'literary fiction' into which his novels have been slotted, claiming an intention to write with more breadth about human experience than is encompassed in that category. *Staring at the Sun*, he claims, was at least in part a reaction against the 'literary' tag, for it is ' "a book in which no one reads books" ' (Kastor B9). Even less intent on penetrating some rarefied sphere of high art, the four detective novels that Barnes published in the 1980s under the *nom de plume* Dan Kavanagh are content to inhabit the violent underbelly of English society and to feature the hard-boiled Duffy, who is much more familiar with Soho's unsavoury sex trade and criminal activities of every stripe than he is with the artistic productions of Marcel Proust or Pablo Picasso. None of the fictions that Barnes has published under his own name strives for some model of artistic purity or the 'high seriousness' that Arnold deemed requisite for truly great literature (*Poetry and Criticism* 325); they tend to be, rather, marked at intervals by self-deflating humour and characterized by generic mongrelism. Erudite but not stuffy, Barnes writes, in Mark Lawson's words, 'like the teacher of your dreams: jokey, metaphorical across both popular and unpopular culture, epigrammatic' ('Short History' 34). What especially cuts against the grain of Barnes's devotion to 'high' culture is his writing style. His diction, which characteristically collapses different levels, intermingles learned and demotic words. Barnes says that he has been influenced in this respect by English literature in general and Shakespeare in particular: 'Shakespeare is nothing if not a mixer of genres, and a mixer of forms of rhetoric, and a mixer of prose and poetry, and a mixer of high and low, and a mixer of farce and tragedy. So it's always been there in our literary culture' (Freiburg 62).

Barnes's restless fictional experimentation has led critics to identify his work as postmodernist, a designation that applies more completely to some of his novels than to others, in which his approach is more straight forwardly realist. His frequent combining of different discursive forms and modes, referred to above, is, as Malcolm Bradbury states, one characteristic of postmodernism that typified much of the fiction published in Britain in the 1980s (407). The dense intertextuality of his novels and stories is also an attribute of postmodernism, one that bespeaks the impossibility of complete artistic originality and establishes the writer as a *bricoleur* whose task is largely to work creatively with received and recycled cultural materials. Vanessa Guignery mentions three other specific respects in which Barnes's fiction may be considered postmodernist: 'he both resorts to and subverts realistic strategies; his writing is essentially self-reflexive; and he celebrates the literary past but also considers it with irony' (*Fiction* 1).

His fictional self-consciousness is manifested in those passages in some of his novels in which the narrators discuss the artistic strategies being employed or otherwise flaunt the artifices behind the illusions of reality that have been put in place. What Alison Lee says about *Flaubert's Parrot* also holds true for some of his other fictions: '[t]hrough metafictional techniques the novel creates levels of fiction and "reality" and questions the Realist assumption that truth and reality are absolutes. *Flaubert Parrot* is typical of contemporary metafictional texts in that, while it challenges Realist conventions, it does so, paradoxically, from within precisely those same conventions' (3). His metafictional games imply that truth is elusive; they suggest that not only his own fictions but also all attempts to represent experience are in some sense fabrications or constructions, not simple presentations of reality. Barnes's work communicates the often-cited 'incredulity towards metanarratives' that for Jean-François Lyotard defines the postmodern condition of contemporary culture and knowledge (xxiv).

It is not only the literary past mentioned by Guignery that Barnes's fictions incorporate by means of intertextuality. Some of them, such as *A History of the World in 10½ Chapters*, are more broadly historical in that they both contain narratives set in past eras and incorporate philosophical commentary on the difficulties that vex any attempts to reconstruct and preserve history. Books such as *Flaubert's Parrot* and *A History of the World in 10½ Chapters* are examples of what Linda Hutcheon calls 'historiographic metafiction': 'novels which are both intensely self-reflexive and yet paradoxically also lay claim to historical events and personages' (*Poetics* 5). Whereas traditional historical novels sustain the pretence of supplying direct access to the past in all of its fullness and particularity, historiographic metafiction periodically undermines the authority of its own representations by exposing their fictive status. As Brian McHale says, whereas traditional historical novels 'typically involve some violation of ontological boundaries', they 'strive to suppress these violations, to hide the ontological "seams" between fictional projections and real world facts'. It is, of course, just these 'seams' that are deliberately on display in postmodern historical fiction (16–17).

Barnes's penchant for fictional experimentation is one of the reasons that critics have applied the adjective 'cosmopolitan' to his writings. Richard Brown, for example, states that 'this prolific writer's most successful experiments in literary form can be most closely compared to [those of] his Italian, French, and South American contemporaries' (68). His internationalism was established not only by his narrative innovations but also by his use of French models and his focus on France as a subject within his novels and stories. In what Bradbury refers to as 'the era of "Europe,"' in which 'European subject matter [is] ever more important' (413), Barnes has frequently used France as a locale for his fictions, and he has even set one of them, *The Porcupine*, in a fictionalized version of Bulgaria and peopled it entirely with Bulgarian characters. William Leith explains that English novelists' new fascination with foreign countries is, at least in part, a corollary of England's waning importance, as both a world power and a literary landscape. Writing in 1993, Leith quotes Barnes as saying that England has become less important than the United States as a fictional subject: 'there's no point in doing a little-England version of the American novel—the Empire is long dead. What is London the centre of in the world? Symphony orchestras, maybe. Symphony orchestras and royalty. But that doesn't make me want to write a novel about the Royal Family . . . ' (14). Hindsight makes one immediately want to qualify these remarks by saying that, in the last decade or so, London and England have remained viable, even fertile, subjects and settings for fiction and also that Barnes *has* gone on, in *England, England,* to write about the Royals, at least in a fantastic, satirical vein. But it remains true today that his orientation is international, not exclusively British. Leith quotes him as saying that 'I don't exactly think of myself as an *English* novelist, but as a novelist. . . . [M]y principal attachment is to the language, rather than the place' (13).

Barnes's main allegiance as a novelist may well be to his native language, which he employs superbly to achieve a wide range of effects, but he is also fluent in French. He is at home in France, which he refers to as 'my other country' (Swanson 3); there, he is a celebrated author who has been given several awards and honours. He has recently translated Alphonse Daudet's *In the Land of Pain* from French into English, but the French writer to whom he is most devoted is Gustave Flaubert, on whom Barnes has written extensively in both *Flaubert's Parrot* and *Something to Declare*. It is not surprising that Flaubert's writing has served as something of a model for Barnes's own, since he considers Flaubert 'the writer's writer *par excellence*, the saint and martyr of literature, the perfector of realism, the creator of the modern novel with *Madame Bovary*, and ... the assistant creator of the modernist novel with *Bouvard et Pécuchet*' (*Something to Declare* xiv). Despite living in a different century when '[w]e no longer believe that language and reality "match up" so congruently' (*Flaubert's Parrot* 88), Barnes shares the commitment that Flaubert had to *le mot juste*, to the precise deployment of individual words in the creation of a style that is perfectly suited for the job at hand. What Barnes's narrator, Geoffrey Braithwaite, says of Flaubert in *Flaubert's Parrot* applies also to Barnes's own goal as a writer: 'Style is not imposed on subject-matter but arises from it. ... The correct word, the true phrase, the perfect sentence are always "out there" somewhere; the writer's task is to locate them by whatever means he can' (88). 'Style', Barnes has said, 'is central. People who don't understand style think it is like a coat of gloss paint applied to the story to make it shine. That's nonsense. Style, form, theme, all pull equally to convey the truth of life' (Vianu 4).

Like Flaubert, Barnes makes masterful use of free indirect discourse to generate both sympathetic understanding of some of his characters and irony at their expense. The technique of free indirect discourse is an outgrowth of his belief, shared with Flaubert, 'that the novelist should be in his work as God is in the universe, everywhere present and nowhere visible' (Vianu 5). This impersonality and invisibility makes his narrators capable of merging successively with several of his characters, occupying their mental and emotional lives. The narrative report that results from this intimate bonding combines features of first-person direct discourse and third-person indirect discourse. It allows readers to become intimately familiar with, and thus sympathetic to, the lives of those characters. But Chris Baldick observes that free indirect discourse, which is to this day still associated with Flaubert, also allows for the generation of irony (87–8). Like his master, whose *Dictionnaire des Idées Reçues* is described in the following quotation, Barnes is a consummate ironist capable not only of broad effects but of subtle gradations: 'Flaubert's dictionary offers a course in irony: from entry to entry, you can see him applying it in various thicknesses, like a cross-channel painter darkening the sky with another wash' (*Flaubert's Parrot* 87).

The arresting simile at the end of the last sentence introduces another literary talent that Barnes shares with Flaubert: a gift for enlivening his writing and emphasizing ideas or descriptive passages with memorable, sometimes shocking, metaphoric language. The figures of speech of both writers are often epigrammatic in their conciseness and wit. Here is one example from Flaubert's work chosen from a long catalogue compiled by Braithwaite: 'What an awful thing life is, isn't it? It's like soup with lots of hairs floating on the surface. You have to eat it nevertheless' (34).

In addition to their common narrative strategies and stylistic propensities, there are intertextual links in two of Barnes's novels that reveal specific borrowings from Flaubert. In an interview, Barnes discloses that he intended Geoffrey Braithwaite and his late, sexually unfaithful wife, Ellen, to parallel Charles and Emma Bovary, although, as Barnes says, Geoffrey is much more intelligent than Charles (McGrath 23). And although Ellen displayed Emma's recklessness, Geoffrey tells us pointedly in defence of her that 'she never ran up bills' (164). Barnes is obviously inviting readers here to contrast this bit of information with their memories of Emma's uncontrolled shopping sprees in Flaubert's novel. Brown points out that the balanced, tripartite structure of Barnes's first novel, *Metroland*, recalls that of Flaubert's *L'Éducation Sentimental* (68), and Guignery notices that when Christopher returns to England he is reading Flaubert's novel (*Fiction* 13). Just as Frédéric Moreau misses the bloody insurrection of 1848 while he is away from Paris visiting Fontainebleau with his lover, Rosanette, so Christopher Lloyd during his stay in Paris is so absorbed in his love affair with Annick that he is oblivious to *les événements* of 1968, the student demonstrations that rocked France politically.

Notwithstanding Barnes's reverence for Flaubert and his own intimate knowledge of the language and culture of France, he claims

that the warm reception given to his work there is not owing to
his having been adopted by the French as one of their own writers.
' "No, no, no," French people have told him. "We like you because
you're . . . so English." ' Although Barnes finds the literary genealogy proposed by these French readers—*Tristram Shandy*, Edward
Lear, Monty Python, Julian Barnes'—to be 'very bizarre indeed'
(Webb 2), he has acknowledged specifically English influences on
his writing. Perhaps surprisingly, these are not the novelists whom
he most admires (Evelyn Waugh, Graham Greene, and Ford Madox
Ford), but the modern poets Thomas Hardy, A. E. Housman, and
Philip Larkin, whose melancholy and pessimistic view of life's
bleakness matches his own:

> there is probably a pervasive melancholy in a lot of what I write. I think
> that this partly comes from the objective assessment of the human
> condition, the inevitability of extinction—and also from an objective
> look at how many people's lives turn out and how rarely achievement
> matches intention. And I recognize such pessimism in the sorts of
> English writer whom I like and admire. (Freiburg 51)

Like Hardy, who 'Never Expected Much' from life (452), and Larkin,
who was 'The Less Deceived' because he doubted that his deepest
hopes could be realized, Barnes, presumably, is steeled against life's
disappointments by his jaundiced view of its possibilities.

It is not only our broadly human condition that has elicited
Barnes's concern. He has also written in response to particular
political and social changes that have taken place within Britain
over the four decades during which he has been writing fiction.
Bradbury discusses the most notable of these changes, the radical metamorphosis of Britain during the 1980s Thatcher decade
and the abrasive effects on society of a new entrepreneurial ethos
that 'introduced a new discourse founded on myths of money' and
killed the post-war consensus that had supported the existence
of the welfare state (396). For Philip Tew, the Thatcher revolution
bifurcates the post-war period, which he therefore argues to be
a less uniform context for the study of British fiction than literary historians usually assume to be the case (56–7). Dominic Head
argues that one effect on both the social and the literary landscape of these dramatic changes has been the creation of a new,

dispossessed underclass (73) and an alteration of the traditional class structure of British society: '[t]he nature of what it means to be "middle class" is transformed in the post-war years, generating a crisis of identity no less problematic than that which surrounds working-class experience, and post-war novelists have not left the contradictions of middle-class experience unremarked' (75). Tew critiques Head's analysis of this crisis of middle-class identity by arguing that he ignores the anti-progressive, politically reactionary form that it takes in the works of many middle-class novelists (67). Tew goes on to state that 'bourgeois intellectuals began to apply the notion of everything breaking down and of the fragmentary to the world as a whole rather than to the hegemonic system they had lost' (70). Tew makes an important point, but it needs to be qualified. Surely, given the very real ecological and military threats that confront even the most prosperous groups in Western democracies, the sense of apocalypse that many novelists communicate is more than a masked expression of their own threatened loss of middle-class privilege. Referring specifically to the decade in which Barnes began to publish his novels, Bradbury states that

> the apocalyptic note became a familiar feature of Eighties fiction in which the culture was random and 'junk,' time frequently dislocated, and oppressive hints of disaster and crisis seemed universal. The sense of recent history as a sequence of past disasters pointing to some further coming catastrophe . . . intensified, multiplied, came closer. (410)

The apocalyptic note is often sounded in Barnes's fiction, and the identity crisis mentioned above is expressed in a number of different ways. In Mira Stout's strikingly metaphoric formulation, 'his work excavates the paved surface of middle-class life and leaves behind unsettling craters' (3). Barnes would concur with Nick Hornby's remark that 'the white south of England middle-class Englishman and woman is the most rootless creature on earth' (*Fever Pitch* 47), for Barnes confided to Stout that 'I grew up in a place [Northwood, a suburb of London] that looks like a settled community but is in fact full of rootless people. You have this psychic rootlessness, which is characteristic of how we are' (7). This deracination is explored in his first novel, *Metroland*, which narrates Christopher Lloyd's attempts to escape the drearily bourgeois routines of his parents' life by becoming an aesthete and embarking on a love affair in the exotic locale of Paris, only to find himself as an adult back, with his own English wife and family, in London's suburbs, his commitment to the bohemian lifestyle of the artist compromised by the materialistic preoccupations of middle-class existence. The conflict between artistic and monetary values also figures in *Talking It Over* and its sequel, *Love, etc.*, love triangles in which the 'sensitive', Wildean Oliver is ultimately bested by the philistine, financially savvy Stuart, who seems a veritable embodiment of Thatcherite principles. The commodification of culture and the triumph of Bradbury's 'new discourse based on money' is demonstrated in even more exaggerated form in *England, England*, in which all of England's history and culture is reduced to nothing more than a one-dimensional, Disneyfied, marketable product on the Isle of Wight. This novel registers the loss of depth and authenticity suffered by English national identity in an era of 'junk' culture and postmodernist simulation.

The inadequacy of middle-class morality to restrain savage impulses is displayed in the fate of *Before She Met Me*'s Graham Hendrick, a mild-mannered, thoroughly 'decent' historian who, in the throes of uncontrollable jealousy, brutally stabs his friend Jack Lupton to death before cutting his own throat with the same knife. The novel bears comparison with Conrad's *Heart of Darkness* and Golding's *Lord of the Flies* as a testament to the superficiality and weakness of civilization in the face of atavistic human instincts and passions. Although Barnes's novel lacks the dystopian, futuristic settings of Ian McEwan's *The Child in Time* or Martin Amis's *London Fields*, *Before She Met Me*, with its macabre, graphically depicted violence, has similarly grotesque features. All three texts are participants in the same Gothic revival that Bradbury analyses in a number of novels written in the 1980s (410–12).

Violence is also a hallmark of the Duffy novels. 'The day they cut Mrs. McKechnie, not much else happened in West Byfleet' (7), reads the first sentence of *Duffy*, and the novel's entire first chapter is devoted to a dramatization of this vicious assault on a defenceless woman by paid thugs, who have invaded her home. *Fiddle City* contains one scene in which a criminal elicits information from Duffy by twisting the gold stud that he wears in one of his ear lobes with a pair of pliers and another, later scene of torture, in which

Duffy first handcuffs the man who has abused him to a chair and then beats him and threatens to inject a lethal amount of heroin into his arm. Duffy's socially marginal position as a bisexual, disgraced ex-policeman—his requisite 'alienation and estrangement' as a private investigator in the hard-boiled American tradition of Raymond Chandler (Moseley 37)—perhaps expresses Barnes's own sense of disaffection from what his detective novels depict as 'a corrupt, brutal, racist, intolerant society' (Guignery *Fiction* 31). As Head states, in a context in which 'an encompassing social vision has become increasingly difficult to sustain in the post-consensus era', it becomes natural to 'focus on marginal and dispossessed figures' (38).

One way for novelists to compensate for this felt loss of social solidarity is by conjuring up imaginatively earlier periods when (at least in the nation's mythology, if not in reality) Britain was more unified and purposeful. As Randall Stevenson says, a 'country experiencing the end of empire, uncertainty in its role abroad, and radical change in its social structure at home could hardly resist looking back on periods of national life apparently more successful and secure than the present' (49). Some of Barnes's novels do resurrect earlier eras, but any nostalgia that they thereby indulge in is undercut with irony. *Staring at the Sun*, for example, dramatizes the years leading up to and during the Second World War, but it resists any temptation that Barnes might have felt to draw on the familiar narrative of the British people's wartime endurance and plucky resistance to German naval and aerial assaults. As Stevenson says, '[f]or some writers the commitment and common purpose of the war years did contribute to forms of nostalgia' (53), but what Barnes's novel focuses on is the growing disillusionment of his protagonist, Jean Serjeant, with her lot in life as a young wife in the heavily patriarchal England of the 1940s. By conventional standards, the one character who is shown in actual combat, the pilot Tommy Prosser, is a coward. The only unequivocal display of courage in the novel—that shown by Jean when she abandons her marriage—has nothing to do with the war effort. *Staring at the Sun* is hardly a heroic or even attractive fictional portrait of the British nation under siege.

Barnes's most recent book, *Arthur & George*, recreates a time that for several decades has been synonymous in the collective literary imagination with innocence and social stability: the Edwardian period, which Bradbury refers to as 'that wonderland before the twentieth century went so wrong' (432). Perhaps Barnes sees the first decade of the century as something of a golden time for fiction as well, for he seems to take pleasure in *Arthur & George* in imitating the form and texture of the Edwardian novel, luxuriating in its generally slower pace, greater density, and more formal prose rhythms. But far from celebrating the years just prior to the First World War as a glorious idyll when everyone knew his or her place in society, Barnes presents early-twentieth-century British society, under its ostensibly peaceful surface, as beset with class and racial animosities, plagued by widespread uncertainties and fears, and menaced by violence. Earlier versions of current social dilemmas are discernible in this text, and it could, therefore, be argued that Barnes is, at least to some extent, using his Edwardian narrative to address contemporary anxieties. What Bradbury says in this regard about the works of a number of contemporary novelists could certainly be applied to *Arthur & George*: 'it was less that novelists were returning to the fictional verities of the past than making the relations of past and present narratives a matter for self-conscious literary examination' (406). And that self-consciousness is another factor which undermines nostalgia in Barnes's treatment of his century-old historical setting, inasmuch as his postmodernist scepticism about the foundational status of metanarratives applies to his own representations of the past. Less obviously a historiographic metafiction than is *Flaubert's Parrot*, *Arthur & George* nevertheless sensitizes observant readers to the fictive nature of its own apparently solid Edwardian social milieu.

One other ideal of Englishness that Barnes's fiction incorporates only to subvert is the pastoral one of a rooted, traditional society existing in harmony with nature's laws. 'A mainstay of poetic imagination', says Stevenson, 'nature in England [has] long been equated with the nature *of* England, and with its supposedly everlasting qualities, yet it [seems] more and more menaced by change and decay' (3). Given a context, then, in which, as Head states, 'the demise of the Nature novel might seem an established fact of literary history' (189), it is not surprising that, in the last section of *England, England*, irony suffuses Barnes's depiction of Anglia, his fantasized version of a future England that has reverted to a pre-industrial, 'organic' condition. What is surprising, though, is that Stevenson seems to miss this irony entirely when he says that *England, England* 'retains strong historical sympathies of its own, largely for supposedly straightforward, bygone decencies of life in the English countryside' (48). Head is more astute in noticing that 'the artificiality of this [allegedly natural] village life is insisted upon' (121). I agree with Head that Anglia does offer its inhabitants some positive qualities (121), and it is certainly preferable to the shrunken, corporate version of England built by Sir Jack Pitman on the Isle of Wight, but Anglia is nevertheless a bogus society whose manufactured 'traditions' reflect ignorance of real English history.

It remains for me here to introduce briefly themes, ideas, and topics in Barnes's fiction that will be analysed more fully in subsequent chapters. He has obsessive concerns that recur from book to book, despite the fact that he is an artist who takes pride in not repeating himself. Merritt Moseley is certainly right to say that 'his books have resisted categorization and defied expectations to a remarkable degree. Each one is markedly different from the ones that have preceded it' (1). But each one is also a new attempt to explore old areas of enquiry and to resolve old dilemmas. Barnes is, after all, a quester, and his novels are vehicles of discovery. As Matthew Pateman says, they 'are all searching for ways of knowing the world . . . ; they all have characters who are striving for some way of finding meaning in an increasingly depoliticized, secularized, localized, and depthless world' (*Julian Barnes* 2). Barnes's interests are, in broad terms, epistemological and ethical. His books ask how, in the absence of absolutes, we can know who we are. How can we know what is true or real, and how, given the labyrinthine treacheries of language, can we accurately communicate what we think we know? Rudolf Freiburg states that the 'questions Barnes does not tire to ask circle round the issues of identity, history, and truth' (43–4). Being acutely sensitive to the vagaries of memory as a human faculty and to the omissions, partisan distortions, and downright fabrications that mar the historical record, Barnes is highly doubtful that humans can represent either their own personal pasts or the collective ones of their nations with anything approaching objective accuracy.

His novels ask not only what we can know but also how we should live and what we can live for. These are ethical concerns, and Barnes has on at least one occasion identified himself as a moralist (McGrath 23). What kinds of experiences and relationships can give life meaning and significance? Can they serve as 'a position from which judgements can be made' (Pateman, *Julian Barnes* 3), a foundation, in other words, for a system of ethics that can order our lives and answer the problem of mortality? Barnes has confessed that he has been troubled by death for most of his life: 'I've been thinking about it for a very long time. I think about it most days of my life. I have since I was 16. . . . I don't get anywhere with it. I don't come up with any answers. But I suppose it must inform the way I live and write' (O'Regan 2). This admission of failure discloses something that is evident to readers of his fiction: the 'moralist' tag fits Barnes only in the sense that he delves into the complications and contradictions that bedevil human existence, not in the sense that he proposes or prescribes a specific code of behaviour. As Moseley says, '[a]s a modern liberal thinker, aware of complexity, he writes books richer in the exploration of serious ideas than in the delivery of finality and doctrinaire answers' (16).

'Parenthesis', the personal essay that serves as the half chapter in *A History of the World in 10½ Chapters*, identifies three potential sources of illumination and redemption: religion, art, and love; and many of Barnes's novels investigate the extent to which any of these can counteract the miseries of life and the grim finality of death. Since most of what he writes about organized religion mocks its absurdities and parodies its texts, it is consistent of him in 'Parenthesis' to reject it out of hand: 'Religion has become either wimpishly workaday, or terminally crazy, or merely businesslike—confusing spirituality with charitable donations' (242). Barnes, whose non-believing parents did not raise him as a church-going Christian, has said, 'I had no faith to lose, only a resistance (which felt more heroic than it was) to the mild regimen of God-referring that an English education entailed' ('Past Conditional' 64). Nevertheless, he has said, rather wistfully, that

> I don't believe in God, but I miss Him. Sometimes, when you see great religious art, or you listen to a great choral work, which is a religious work, you think how wonderful it would have been to have been alive when these things were being painted or composed, and to believe it all. (O'Regan 2)

As the last sentence implies, art is for Barnes something of a link to divinity, or at least to the tenuous afterlife of divinity in a scientific, secular age. As I said earlier in this introductory chapter, aestheticism obviously has a great appeal for him, since the refinements and rewards of artistic experience are recurring topics in his fiction. As Peter Childs says, 'belief in the supremacy of art' is frequently voiced by characters in Barnes's narratives (86). It is no accident that Flaubert, his favourite novelist, was also an aesthete. But, as Barnes reveals at certain points in his fiction, art is flawed as a surrogate religion. It may outlast its creators, but it is not eternal; not impervious to the ravages of time, change, and decay. And, in any event, although great art may continue to exert its appeal for millennia, this is not the same as the promise of personal immortality that religion once offered. The speaker of 'Parenthesis' rejects art as a faith, however reluctantly, for its experience 'isn't accessible to all, or where accessible isn't always inspiring or welcome. So religion and art must yield to love. It gives us our humanity, and also our mysticism' (243).

In one fashion or another, all of Barnes's novels deal with love, in at least some of its many varieties. 'Parenthesis' extols love, associating it not only with our humanity and mysticism, but also with imaginative acuity and truth itself: 'Love makes us see the truth, makes it our duty to tell the truth' (238). Yet, as I argue in Chapter 5, his fictions actually reveal love to be nebulous, volatile, and undependable, not a secure basis for determining what is true and what is false. Love certainly animates and drives his characters, but more often than not it is a source of emotional turmoil and misery for them, not of self-definition, moral guidance, and happiness. In the tradition of the nineteenth-century European novels, Barnes frequently spins narratives of suspicion, jealousy, and betrayal. Moseley states that 'connected with [his] interest in marriage is the subject of infidelity and adultery, or cuckoldry. Barnes's male protagonists are often the victims of their wives' infidelity, though his subtlety in his approach makes "victim" seem far too crude a concept' (13–14). Indeed, in the case of *Before She Met Me*, the protagonist, Graham Hendrick, can hardly be considered his wife's victim at all, since she is never sexually unfaithful to him. His jealousy is actually retrospective, since he becomes obsessed not with any current lovers but with the men in her life before she met him.

Although his books are informed by pessimism, the experience of reading them is far from dispiriting. They are richly textured, aesthetically accomplished, highly entertaining productions, fuelled by clear-sighted intelligence, crackling wit, emotional depth, and a broad imaginative sympathy. Julian Barnes may be a reticent, impersonal presence in most of his books, but the impressive creative power that makes him a major author is on display in all of them.

2

LIFE AND WORK

In *Flaubert's Parrot* Geoffrey Braithwaite makes an analogy between a biography and a fishing net, which could, 'with no great injury to logic', be defined as 'a collection of holes tied together with string'. He elaborates as follows: '[t]he trawling net fills, then the biographer hauls it in, sorts, throws back, stores, fillets and sells. Yet consider what he doesn't catch: there is always far more of that' (38). Most of the subject's thoughts, feelings, and experiences escape through the holes, and therefore the finished biography, no matter how scrupulous and capacious, will inevitably fall well short of its goal of capturing and preserving an individual's life with fidelity in the web of language. Consequently, I make no great claims for the adequacy of the biographical sketch of Julian Barnes that follows. I do trust, however, that, like the 'shilling life' of the emotionally weak 'great man' in Auden's 'Who's Who', which supplies 'all the facts' (109), this section will at least give readers who are new to Barnes's work some salient information about his life and career as a writer.

Although he was born in Leicester (on 19 January 1946), and supports that city's football team, Barnes is actually a Londoner. While he was still an infant, his parents, Albert and Kaye Barnes, moved to the suburb of Acton and then, ten years later, to Northwood, which is part of 'Metroland', the vast suburban area served by the London Underground's Metropolitan Line. From 1957 to 1964, he commuted on the train in order to attend the prestigious City of London School. He has said that the first third or so of *Metroland* is an autobiographical narrative of what his life was like then as a schoolboy (Vianu 3). With sensitivity and wit, it registers the emotional ups and downs of his artistically minded protagonist as he

28

shuttles between the banal setting of his family's home and the more glamorous space of inner London where his school is located. The novel makes it clear that Christopher is bored by the suburbs, but, even so, it is a bit surprising to learn how extreme and confused Barnes's feelings are about where he grew up: '"Well, I quite liked it at the time. I mean, I didn't hate it I don't think," he says cautiously. "Yeah, maybe I did. . . . I did hate it. That's true; I loathed it"' (Stout 2). Needless to say, he now lives in a more central—and more fashionable—area of North London.

Barnes's parents, now deceased, raised him and his older brother, Jonathan, in what Stout calls 'a typically English spirit of sound middle-class caution, stability, and routine (achingly well evoked in *Metroland*)' (7). 'I can't remember a row between my parents—ever', he told Stout. 'They were very English, controlled, certainly not given to spontaneous or extravagant gestures' (7). He has said that he 'didn't mind [their emotional reserve]. . . . That seemed normal. I don't mind it in retrospect either' (Summerscale 2). He claims to prefer the 'tradition of English emotional reticence which can easily fall away into emotional inexpressiveness and frigidity . . . to the Oprahfication of the emotions, which is what has happened. People talking about their emotional lives in staggering detail on Celebrity Love Island is so banal' (Thorpe 2). Since most of his interviewers comment on Barnes's own self-contained, aloof demeanour, it is safe to assume that he learned early on to follow his parents' example. He has said that

> [t]emperamentally, I have a lot in common with my father. I don't like argument. I like argument on the printed page, but argument as a way of having a friendship or a relationship with somebody—I've never been able to do that. I would retreat into silence rather than argue and rage and storm. (Summerscale 1)

His friends have commented approvingly on his reticence:

> 'Julian is like all interesting people,' says [novelist] Ian McEwan. 'It takes a long time to get to know him. I have a sense of a man with a rich life and not all of it's on show and that's great.' . . . Another old friend, biographer Hermione Lee, calls Barnes 'a quite silent person.' She explains, 'There's always something going on that you might not know about'. (Begley 88)

Barnes might well admire and share his parents' tendency not to wear their hearts on their sleeves, but it is also clear that when he was growing up he needed more emotional support from them than they were capable of giving him. Their very English reserve did, in his words quoted above, 'fall away' into something approaching 'frigidity'. When, for example, as a teenager he rushed into the house excitedly to announce that he had been accepted with a scholarship to Magdalene College, Oxford, his mother could only reply, 'Yes, we thought that's what [the letter] was' (Stout 7). There were no effusive expressions of congratulation or celebratory gestures. His parents' conversation, hemmed in by proprieties and prohibitions, 'reduced Julian and his brother Jonathan to "a sort of stunned boredom" as children' (Herbert 1). Barnes told Summerscale, rather poignantly, that 'I suppose I wish my father had told me he loved me, but you just . . . assume that. You have to assume that' (3). Barnes had more affection for his father than for his self-centred, domineering, talkative mother, who eclipsed her husband, reducing his relationship with his son to 'an occasional wink or glance'. Barnes has said that she was 'always there . . . nattering, organizing, fussing, controlling. . . . [N]one of the men in the family were . . . how shall I put it? None of us were relentlessly macho or dominating, so she didn't have much opposition, you could say' (Summerscale 1). When the novelist-to-be was a boy, his mother once criticized him for having ' "too much imagination." . . . She criticized his first novel as a "bombardment" of filth and would show her friends the cover but not allow them to look inside' (Herbert 1). It is little wonder that Barnes has confessed that 'I don't feel any great sense of family loyalty. . . . I never have' (Summerscale 3).

It was his parents who introduced him to France as a child on family vacations, beginning in 1959, but readers might be surprised to learn that he found these early excursions to what would become his beloved second country less than idyllic:

> Those early holidays were filled with anxiety (would anyone understand a word I said? would my father get ratty in the heat? would we fail to find a hotel room with twin beds, since my brother, no doubt for good reason, declined to bunk down with me?) Later, in the long silent quarrel and faux existentialism of late adolescence, I took against my parents'

values and therefore against their love of France. At university I gave up
languages for philosophy, found myself ill-equipped for it, and returned
reluctantly to French. In my twenties, other countries appealed to me
more. (*Something to Declare* xii)

Only when he was in his thirties did he fully embrace France (xii),
although before then he did choose to spend a year alone in France.
During 1966–67, he taught 'English conversation and English civilization' at a school in Rennes (19). Barely older than some of his
pupils, he struggled as a teacher, desperately

> devising various strategies to keep them quiet and avoid the glow-
> ering irruption into the classroom of the *surveillant général,* an
> ex-Algerian war veteran who terrified me even more than he did the
> boys. I'm not sure how reliably English civilization was depicted in our
> conversations—I remember being grilled about London night clubs
> (I bluffed tremendously) and London girls (ditto); though I would
> become more plausibly authoritative on the key cultural question of
> that time, whether or not the Beatles would break up. (19–20)

His brother, who has taught Philosophy at the Sorbonne in Paris, as
well as at Oxford and Geneva universities, is also a Francophile. He
currently lives in France.

Their father considered Jonathan, a future university don, to be
the cleverer of the two brothers (Summerscale 1), but Julian did
excel as a student of Modern Languages at Oxford, from where he
graduated with a B.A. (honours) in 1968. Readers might imagine
that Barnes's bent for languages—and for French in particular—is
a legacy of his upbringing, since both of his parents were French
teachers. But Barnes does not believe this to be the source of his
passion for language and literature: 'I think that came from reading books rather than from my parents' (Summerscale 1). Whereas
some famous authors have blossomed at university (Tennyson
and Forster come immediately to mind), Barnes did not thrive:
'I suppose I was disappointed that I didn't fall in with a glittering
circle of friends. . . . I think I was probably oppressed by the myth
of Oxford—climbing over the college walls late at night, getting
drunk—but there seemed something rather inauthentic about it'
(Stout 8). Barnes's shyness did not help his social life there; he told
Stout that he had never even attended a party before he went to

university (8). Nor did he discover his vocation at Oxford, because at that point in his life

> the idea of being a writer was something that seemed off the radar. . . . 'I used to go to the English society and examine famous writers like Robert Graves and Stephen Spender who came to speak. I thought it must be wonderful to be a writer. But it was what other people did'. (Wroe 4)

After university, Barnes took the civil service examinations, but, instead of working for the government after being offered the job of tax inspector, he got a position as a lexicographer with the Oxford English Dictionary Supplement. His task was 'to predate new coinages or usages, sitting in the Bodleian [Library], speed-reading hundreds of books for appearances of the word sought' (Lawson 'Short History' 36). He specialized in 'rude words and sports words' (Smith 73). He has said that his three-year stint with the OED made him 'less prescriptive about language. And also less old farty and valetudinarian and pessimistic'. It saved him from the common belief that language use is degenerating and that 'the barbarians are at the gates' (Birnbaum 'Robert Birnbaum' 5). Recognizing that language's constant state of flux is not a cause for anxiety might have emboldened him as a writer to use words more innovatively and creatively. After working as a lexicographer, Barnes studied law and was actually accepted to the Bar in 1974, but he never practised as a barrister. He has said, though, that his legal training served him in good stead when he came to write the courtroom scenes in *Arthur & George* (Lewis 9).

Instead of becoming a lawyer, he decided to throw all of his energies into freelance journalism, which he had already been doing part-time. He wrote book reviews for the *TLS* and articles for several other different periodicals, over time working and becoming friends with some of the leading writers of his generation: the late Ian Hamilton, Craig Raine, James Fenton, Christopher Hitchens, Clive James, and Martin Amis, whom he worked under at *The New Statesman*. During the 1970s, Barnes served as contributing editor with the *New Review*, assistant literary editor with the *New Statesman*, and deputy literary editor with the *Sunday Times*. As Edward Pygge, he wrote the Greek Street column for the *New Review*, and taking the name Basil Seal from a character in Evelyn Waugh's fiction, he reviewed restaurants for the *Tatler*. He was also a television critic first for the *New Statesman* and then for the *Observer*, where he replaced Clive James. He resigned from this position in 1986, after four years:

> By that time, not only are you fed up with watching television, but you're fed up with your own opinions. If you're writing 50 columns a year, that's 200 columns, at 1200 words, which is a quarter of a million words on television if you add it up—and you try *not* to add it up until you've resigned the column. (Kastor B9)

In 1979, Barnes married Pat Kavangh, who was to become a very successful literary agent. Both of the public scandals in which Barnes has been caught up have involved her. The first was her widely known love affair in 1989 with the writer Jeanette Winterson, who is said to have written a heavily fictionalized account of their relationship in her 1992 novel *Written on the Body* ('Jeanette Winterson 1959– '). According to Stout, although Barnes was deeply hurt by his wife's infidelity, the two worked hard to repair their marriage (9). The second scandal was his very public falling out with Martin Amis in the mid-1990s, after Amis dropped Kavanagh as his literary agent. Amis has written about how Barnes terminated their friendship in a letter punctuated with 'a well known colloquialism. That phrase consists of two words. The words consist of seven letters. Three of them are fs' (Amis, *Experience* 247). Amis says that his reply included the following: 'Jules, tell me to fuck off and everything if you want—but try and stay my friend and try and help me be a friend to Pat . . . I will call you in a while—quite a long while. I'll miss you' (249).

In *Experience*, Amis refers to Barnes as 'uxorious' (247). While the modifier could obviously be applied to a few of Barnes's characters, especially *Before She Met Me*'s Graham Hendrick, it is hard to see how Barnes's loyalty to his wife, who, Amis admits, 'was and is a first-rate agent' (Rusbridger 4), could be fairly construed as evidence that his love for her is excessive. When asked in 2000 whether he is 'still on non-speaking terms with Barnes', Amis replied, ' "No. When we meet, we chat, yes. You know, it's not what it was, but it's . . . " ' (Rusbridger 4). The very private Barnes has refused to comment publicly on either scandal, but, as Thorpe says, 'this reticence has only whetted appetites' (4).

By all accounts, Barnes and Kavanagh have a rich life together. They enjoy travelling, gardening, and entertaining friends. Barnes '"takes his pleasures seriously"', Begley quotes Ian McEwan as saying,

> 'and he knows how to share them'. Several friends, including McEwan, report that Barnes is an excellent cook and a connoisseur of fine wines. Says Hermione Lee, 'He has made a high art out of worldliness.' She adds that Barnes and Kavanagh, who have no children, are also extraordinarily generous—'and they expend their generosity on their friends'. (Begley 88)

Jay McInerney told Stout that '[t]hey've created a little kingdom . . . the garden, the wine cellar, the kitchen, and the guest book where visitors draw self-caricatures. It's almost too good to be true. I don't know—they make a great case for childlessness' (9). When asked whether he regrets not fathering an offspring, Barnes replied, 'I've never passionately wanted children but, you know, in those alternative lives that you didn't lead, obviously one would be with children' (Herbert 3).

Barnes was writing fiction in the 1970s, but his first novel, *Metroland*, was not published until 1980, when he was 34. He has said that the novel 'took me seven to eight years from start to finish. Now I look at it and think it was an 18-month book, but I was very lacking in confidence' (Billen 26). Although *Metroland* was hardly a best seller, it had its admirers amongst critics, and it did win a prestigious literary prize: the Somerset Maugham Award for a first novel. *Metroland*, the only novel in Barnes' *oeuvre* that possesses autobiographical elements (Vianu 3), is a *Bildungsroman*. 'If a novelist is going to write a coming-of-age book', says Moseley, 'it is probably going to be the first book. Julian Barnes is no exception' (18).

In 1998, nearly 20 years after its publication, *Metroland* was made into a film by Philip Saville from a screenplay by Adrian Hodge. When Barnes was asked whether he was happy with the result, he dodged the question by making the general statement that '[f]ilm is a radically different medium, and the book should therefore be destroyed and reinvented if it is to be a real film, as opposed to an illustrated adaptation' ('You Ask the Questions: Julian Barnes' 2). In the case of *Metroland*, the filmmakers failed in the task of reinvention, producing instead an illustrated carica-ture that sensationalizes the novel and strips it of subtlety and wit. They did make some structural changes, beginning the narrative with Chris and Marion married in Metroland and then dramatiz-ing the scenes from Chris's school days and his sojourn in Paris as flashbacks. In the process, they gave short shrift to the first section of the novel, set in the early 1960s, in which Chris and Toni are young teenagers. Those scenes lack the sharply observed comedy of the novel and also the irony that is generated in it through Chris's retrospective narration. The same actors who play Chris and Toni as adults (Christian Bale and Lee Ross, respec-tively) were cast to play them as adolescents, and this makes those scenes look unintentionally ridiculous. Bale and Ross, dressed in school uniforms, mug at the camera unconvincingly as they try to impersonate disaffected youth. The section set in Paris is han-dled with more delicacy, inasmuch as Chris's initiation by Annick (strongly portrayed by Elsa Zylberstein) into the mysteries of sex-uality and honesty is depicted with humour and pathos. Emily Watson performs ably throughout as the grounded, clear-sighted Marion, and Bale is creditable in bringing out Chris's ambivalence and bemusement as he struggles to reconcile himself to married life in the suburbs. But the film sensationalizes the book on which it is based at far too many turns. For example, the passage in the third part in which Chris first flirts with a woman at a party and then backs out of having sex with her becomes an obligatory nude scene in the film. Toni acts not just as a provocation to Chris, spurring his dissatisfaction with his bourgeois life, but as a Machi-avellian manipulator who engineers the attempted seduction of his friend at the party. It is not enough in the film that the two men wrangle with each other and debate first principles, as they do in the novel: they must also have a melodramatic fist fight as well. Finally, as one reviewer notes, the film looks terrible: '[t]he whole movie has an uncomfortable intimacy, and the close-ups are lit as unforgivingly as an old Polaroid. (Ross's face, in partic-ular, seems to be shot in terrifying Pore-O-Rama.) The message seems to be: you can go home again, but Jesus, dim the lights' (Elias).

In 1980, the same year that *Metroland* appeared in print, Barnes also published, under the name Dan Kavanagh, the detective novel *Duffy*. Critics have found it more than coincidental that Kavanagh is also his wife's surname. During the 1980s he went on to write three more thrillers with the same protagonist: *Fiddle City* (1981), *Putting the Boot In* (1985), and *Going to the Dogs* (1987). The face-tious thumbnail biographies that Barnes created along with the pseudonym show that we are meant to take neither his alter ego nor the books very seriously. Barnes is signalling that he is engaged in a kind of literary slumming. 'It takes me two [to] three years to write a novel', he has said; 'it used to take me two [to] three weeks to write a thriller. That's about the relative level of importance I accord them' (Vianu 4). He could hardly have been ashamed of them, how-ever, since he did not try very hard to conceal the fact that he was the creator of Duffy. 'I'm not denying [the detective novels] or repu-diating them', he told Robert Birnbaum. 'I think they're quite jolly' (Birnbaum 'Robert Birnbaum Interviews Julian Barnes' 4). Never-theless, in the same interview he said quite firmly that 'I'm not going to write any more. . . . I had an excess of energy at the time, which is why I was doing them, and then I didn't. They were perfectly reasonably successful in their own right, but my books are more successful' (4).

In my Introduction, I cited Moseley's observation that the Duffy novels deploy the conventions of American hard-boiled detective fiction rather than those of the more genteel British tradition (37). Nick Duffy's literary ancestors are Dashiell Hammett's Sam Spade, Raymond Chandler's Philip Marlowe, and John D. MacDonald's Travis McGee, not Agatha Christie's Hercule Poirot. The social and linguistic context for Duffy's adventures, however, is firmly English, not American. Barnes takes readers inside the subcul-tures of London's police and criminal underworld, mimicking the accents and slang heard in those spheres with seeming authen-ticity. As Guignery notices, Barnes's writing in the Duffy novels has 'a blatant oral dimension and a colloquial and even a vul-gar tone' (*Fiction* 32). This stylistic quality is in keeping with the hard-boiled tradition, but Duffy's bisexuality is interestingly at variance with the hyper-masculine ethos of American fictional private eyes. One can readily imagine the loathing that it would generate in a character such as Mike Hammer, the reactionary, brutal protagonist of Micky Spillane.

Each of the Duffy books is set in a different 'world': *Duffy* places its eponymous protagonist in the sleazy milieu of Soho's sex trade; *Fiddle City* takes us inside London's labyrinthine Heathrow Airport, where Duffy encounters drug smugglers and thieves; *Putting the Boot In* introduces readers to the life, both on and off the pitch, of an unheralded professional football team, threatened with relegation as it labours in the Third Division and victimized by a variety of suspicious mishaps, which are the subject of Duffy's investigations; *Going to the Dogs* recreates the sequestered *mise en scène* of classic English detective novels, although it lacks their gentility. In this regard, Guignery perceptively notes that the novel's opening sentence—'There was a body in the video library' (11)—'invokes the title of Agatha Christie's second Miss Marple novel, *The Body in the Library* (1942), thus alluding to English country house detective fiction' (*Fiction* 35). Guignery neglects to say, though, that Barnes's addition of the word 'video' injects irony, for it drains the word that it modifies, 'library', of its traditional associations with literacy and learning. In the corrupt contemporary Britain inhabited by Duffy, the manor house is no longer a metonymy for a civilized way of life that can be restored once the detective identifies the murderer; it is merely an empty shell, an archaic remnant of the past packaged by estate agents as a luxury item for the rich.

In the 27 years following the lengthy gestation period needed for *Metroland*, Barnes has become an efficient, prolific writer of books, having published 19 more of them between 1980 and 2008. And, even though he began to devote more time to fiction in 1986, after his 40th birthday (the day on which he resigned from the *Observer*, finished writing *Staring at the Sun*, and purchased a full-sized snooker table), he never completely stopped writing journalism. '[N]ow it's my fiction that supports my journalism', he told an interviewer, 'not the other way round' (Webb 4). In 1982, he published his second novel, *Before She Met Me*, a darkly comic story of a man's descent into insane, murderous jealousy, and 1984 marked the appearance of what many consider to be his masterpiece, *Flaubert's Parrot*. Whereas neither *Metroland* nor *Before She Met Me* achieved best-seller status, *Flaubert's Parrot*, an unclassifiable mélange of a book about an aging widower's obsession with Flaubert, was wildly successful, both critically and commercially. In England, it did not win the Booker Prize, for which it was nominated, but it did receive the Geoffrey Faber Memorial Prize. In France, it was awarded the *Prix Médicis*. Since none of the many books that he has written subsequently has received quite the acclaim that *Flaubert's Parrot* did, Barnes is sometimes asked if he resents its success. His standard way of answering is to quote Kingsley Amis, who 'was once asked if *Lucky Jim* was an albatross around his neck, and he said it was better than not having a bloody albatross at all. That's my perspective'. Being known for *Flaubert's Parrot* is better than being in the position of never having 'written a book that anyone has ever heard of' (O'Regan 1).

In 1986, Barnes published *Staring at the Sun*, a novel that he had begun writing before he took up *Flaubert's Parrot* (McGrath 23). Upon completing *Flaubert's Parrot*, he resumed work on *Staring at the Sun*, which, after it appeared in due course, disappointed some readers in seeming more conventional and undistinguished than its immediate predecessor. But in combining different genres and in spanning the historical past and an imagined, dystopian future, this narrative of an ordinary woman's struggle to find meaning and freedom in life is not without adventurous experimental features. The book is also original in the way that it makes 'whimsical details as compelling as more freighted events' (Stout 5). As Barnes says, '[a]t first they're just odd stories, but by the end they become metaphors' (McGrath 23).

A History of the World in 10½ Chapters, published in 1989, deals with some of the same themes as *Flaubert's Parrot*, and, in Barnes's original conception, it was to feature the same narrator: 'I had this character in *Flaubert's Parrot*, Geoffrey Brathwaite, a tedious man. It was my idea to make him rewrite the entire Bible. Some of that fed into the first chapter, the Noah one' (qtd. in Cook 10). In the event, Braithwaite suffered the ignominious fate of being supplanted by a woodworm as the tale's narrator. *A History of the World in 10½ Chapters* rivalled *Flaubert's Parrot* in achieving both impressive sales figures and the praise of critics for its formal novelty. Similarly preoccupied with the impossibility of attaining an objective perspective on the historical past, *A History* also defied readers' expectations of what a novel should look like.

A discontinuous agglomeration of different kinds of discourses, the book is a dazzling display of narrative invention, wit, and cleverness.

In *Talking It Over* (1991), Barnes discovered an ingenious formal method for returning to a topic that he had previously addressed in *Metroland* and *Before She Met Me*: jealousy and sexual infidelity. *Talking It Over*, like its sequel *Love, etc.* (2000), is constructed dramatically as a series of juxtaposed monologues, most of which are uttered by the three principal characters, Stuart, Gillian, and Oliver, who form a love triangle. In Brown's astute formulation, *Talking It Over* 'returns to a realistic idiom while deftly absorbing some well-documented trends in the sociology of contemporary love: frankly capitalistic and commercial metaphors; the intensification of romantic affection during a period when marital break-up is almost the norm; background details regarding telephone pornography and AIDS' (69). *Love, etc.*, in which Stuart tries to win Gillian back from Oliver, who had stolen her from him in *Talking It Over*, is darker in tone, since the characters, now a decade older, have become rather disillusioned and embittered by life.

In 1996, a film based on *Talking It Over*, directed and written (in collaboration with Dodine Henry) by Marion Vernoux, was released in France with the title *Love, etc.*, the same one as Barnes's sequel to *Talking It Over*. The potential confusion here is dissipated when one learns that *Love, etc.* was Barnes's original title for *Talking It Over*, which he dropped after he discovered that an American novel called *Love, etc.*, written by Bel Kaufman, was already in print. But, as Guignery explains, 'the French publishers were perfectly happy with the original title, which was retained for the French translation. Ten years later Barnes silenced his qualms and entitled the sequel *Love, etc.*, which proved embarrassing to the French publishers, who named the second volume *Dix Ans Après* [*Ten Years Later*]' (79). Vernoux's film is more successful in Barnes's terms than Saville's *Metroland*, in that it substantially re-imagines the novel and 'translates' Barnes's written text into the conventions of cinema. As mentioned above, the most striking feature of the novel is the narrative technique of monologues delivered directly by the characters to the readers. Since this is essentially a non-dramatic technique, in the sense that it privileges 'telling' over 'showing', it has no cinematic equivalent. But, as Guignery says, Vernoux did find ways to retain the monologue format:

> She used the conventional technique of the voice-over, which helped the characters to comment on what was happening or gave access to their thoughts and feelings. When photos of Gillian and Stuart's marriage are taken, the screen is frozen and each of the three protagonists expresses his/her feelings to the camera one after the other. (83)

Guignery is misleading here in not telling readers that Vernoux has renamed the characters. (Stuart has become Benoit; Oliver, Pierre; and Gillian, Marie; and Gillian's French mother has become Marie's English mother.) But Guignery is insightful in explaining that Vernoux has supplemented the voice-overs with stylized scenes in which Pierre and Benoit speak their thought aloud to strangers, who stand in for the silent reader addressed by the characters in the novel (83).

Some of the lines spoken by the characters in the novel's monologues appear in dialogue in the film, and the characters themselves contrast with each other in similar ways. Benoit, portrayed by Yvan Attal, is somewhat clumsy and lacking in confidence, but he nevertheless seems a more romantic figure than Stuart. Pierre, played by Charles Berling, is true to his original in being annoyingly self-absorbed and verbose, but he seems more conventionally masculine than the effeminate Oliver. Charlotte Gainsbourg's Marie is, like Gillian, straight-forwardly charming. The film also retains many individual details and scenes from the written text. Stuart's cuckoo clock makes an appearance, with its two men dressed for good and bad weather respectively symbolizing the impossibility of both Benoit and Pierre being happy at the same time as figures in a romantic triangle. The characters go to the beach together (although they do not write their names in the sand), Benoit lends Pierre money, and Pierre watches Marie clean and restore paintings. These scenes have a symbolic resonance in the novel that they lack in the film, which, perhaps inevitably, is shorn of the novel's thematic complexity and intellectual weight. Vernoux does not, for example, explore the subjective nature of truth or the conceptual parallel between love and money. Instead, she concentrates on exploiting the dramatic potential of the emotionally explosive situation in which the three characters find themselves. She builds the plot expertly to a climax in which a drunken, angry Benoit, over dinner, confronts his wife and friend with their treachery. As Guigney says, the film differs most from the novel in its ending (84). Whereas the novel concludes with Gillian goading Oliver into an act of violence against her so that Stuart, whom she knows to be nearby in hiding, can witness it, the film ends with the tentative reconciliation of the three principals on the beach at Boulogne as they quietly celebrate the new millennium on 1 January 2000. Guigney states that in Barnes's own judgement, 'the novel's ending is sinister and cruel while the film's conclusion, which may appear rather sentimental, is in fact bitter sweet' (84).

The Porcupine (1992) is unique amongst Barnes's novels in that it had its first publication in a Bulgarian translation, not in its original form in English. This was appropriate inasmuch as the novel is set in a fictionalized, though unnamed, version of Bulgaria. The narrative follows the trial of the country's former dictator, and in the process it tracks the dramatic social changes there following the collapse of the Soviet Union and its satellite communist states. Barnes has said that The Porcupine 'is a political novel about that old but still true problem: the weakness of liberalism confronted by the certainty of a system that believes it has all the answers' (Freiburg 61).

Barnes next published, in 1995, Letters from London, a collection of journalistic pieces that had originally appeared as articles in The New Yorker magazine. Rather than discussing the book at this juncture, however, I wish to deal first with two novels that were more recently published, England, England (1998) and Arthur & George (2005). Then I shall tackle the four non-fiction books (Letters from London, Something to Declare, The Pedant in the Kitchen, and Nothing To Be Frightened Of) and the two collections of short stories (Cross Channel and The Lemon Table).

Like Flaubert's Parrot, both England, England and Arthur & George were nominated for, but did not win, the Booker Prize, which continues to elude Barnes. England, England exposes the vacuity of Thatcher's entrepreneurial capitalism at a time when England's national heritage is nothing more than a collection of commodities to be bought and sold. In Barnes's fantasy, a Rupert Murdoch–style magnate named Sir Jack Pitman replicates what he determines to be the 'Fifty Quintessences of Englishness' on the Isle of Wight (86), which becomes a replacement for England itself as a tourist destination and, indeed, as a nation on the world's stage. *England, England* has farcical and satirical qualities, but *Arthur & George* is uniformly serious in tone, realistic in narrative method, and slower in pace. The novel is based on Britain's historical parallel to France's much better-known Dreyfus Affair: a case of legal injustice in which a solicitor of Indian descent, George Edalji, was convicted of crimes that he patently did not commit. Like the Dreyfus Affair, the Edalji case exposed deep divisions and racial animosities within society, and it also involved a famous writer. Sir Arthur Conan Doyle was Emile Zola's British counterpart as a champion of the victim. Barnes weaves into the narrative of this legal case fictional biographies of his two principal characters.

Letters from London was the happy result of an offer that Barnes received in 1989 to become the new London correspondent of *The New Yorker*. He has said that in accepting it he was assuming the role of 'a foreign correspondent in my own country'. Taken together, the essays in the volume constitute an impressionistic portrait of a Britain responding, not always very well, to various kinds of pressures. For all his even-handed, calm tone, Barnes often slyly builds up details so as to expose the ironies that underlie many of the events and situations that he writes about. As Guignery says, the book adumbrates 'the satirical vein of *England, England*' (*Fiction* 97). One of his essays, 'Fake!', even explores in a preliminary way one of the main topics of *England, England*: the '[p]icturesque fakery . . . [that] is embedded in many aspects of British life' (27). The novel suggests that, in fabricating reality, Sir Jack Pitman is guilty of nothing more than exaggerating a method that is already widely used in Britain. 'The British are good at tradition', says Barnes; 'they're also good at the invention of tradition (from plowman's lunch to the clan tartan). And like any other nation, they aren't too keen on having those invented traditions exposed as bogus' (*Letters* 27).

The subjects that Barnes covers in *Letters from London* are various. For instance, he describes garden mazes, narrates the travails of the Royal Family, reports on the world chess championships, and reflects on the significance of the Channel Tunnel that now connects England and France. But the topic that dominates *Letters from London* is politics. The collection spans the end of the Thatcher years, the surprising ascendancy of John Major and his Conservative Party's defeat of Labour in the 1992 election, and the arrival of Tony Blair on the political scene. What brings the pieces to life is not just his grasp of the issues and the astuteness of his analysis, but more the vividness of his vignettes and his portraits of the politicians, such as Norman Lamont, a former Chancellor of the Exchequer who was involved in a scandal. As Moseley says, Barnes's 'ability to make characters, usually comic, out of such figures as Lamont . . . is a tribute to his novelistic power' (168). He frequently employs his keen wit and his gift for metaphor and analogy to devastating satirical effect.

Like *Letters from London*, *Something to Declare* collects essays that Barnes had originally written as journalistic assignments, in this case, for a variety of different periodicals, not just one. The title's play on words refers not just to consumer goods that English tourists need to declare at customs upon returning from France but also to the author's deep love for his second, adopted country. As Guignery points out, whereas '*Letters from London* dealt mainly with contemporary and political subjects, *Something to Declare*, dedicated to his now deceased parents who were French teachers, is more concerned with culture and the late nineteenth century' (*Fiction* 99). The fifth and sixth essays, 'Tour de France 1907' and 'Tour de France 2000', juxtapose the past and the present, contrasting Edith Wharton's and Henry James's cultivated leisurely exploration of France in an early automobile with the frenetic bicycle race of today, fuelled not by petrol but by amphetamines and steroids. Much of *Something to Declare* is devoted to artists—songwriters and musicians (Boris Vian, Jacques Brel, and Georges Brassens), filmmakers (François Truffaut), painters (Gustave Courbet), and, of course, writers (Georges Simenon, Charles Baudelaire, Stéphane Mallarmé, and, preeminently, Gustave Flaubert). Fully half of the book revisits the subject of *Flaubert's Parrot*: the life of the great novelist and his relations with those in his circle, such as his fellow writer and mistress, Louise Collet, and his niece, Caroline Commanville.

The link between *Something to Declare* and *The Pedant in the Kitchen* is the food writer Elizabeth David, who popularized Mediterranean cuisine in Britain after the Second World War. She is the subject of one of the essays in the former volume and also one of the authorities to whom Barnes defers in the latter book, which records, not principally his love of food, but first and foremost his anxiety as a cook, his finicky need to follow recipes to the letter. As Judy Rumbold observes, this pedantic exactitude is the opposite of the currently popular 'bung-it-all-in-and-see-what-happens approach to cookery, as advocated by Nigella Lawson, Jamie Oliver and Nigel Slater. Not for him the blithe approximations and cavalier slapdashery that has made the whole business of entertaining a much more relaxing affair' (1). Barnes would be unfazed by this criticism, however, since he has a rather low opinion of TV chefs: 'I remain a text-based cook and am broadly suspicious of those persuaded to inflate their personalities in front of the camera' (*Pedant* 13). The book is a rather slight affair, but it does offer amusing anecdotes about some of his culinary triumphs and misadventures.

Barnes's most recent volume, not yet published in North America as I write in the spring of 2008, is *Nothing To Be Frightened Of*, which one commentator describes as 'a disquisition on death that addresses religion, philosophy, literature, identity, memory, evolutionary biology and the nature of the universe' (Summerscale 1). Barnes stresses that the book is not an autobiography (Herbert 2), but in it he does write candidly about his family. 'I'm a novelist', Summerscale quotes him as saying, 'and therefore ideas have to be rooted in people. If I'm going to write about death, I'm not equipped to write a general, theoretical, argumentative, philosophical book about it—that's not how I write. It has to be connected to me and therefore also my parents' (1).

The short fictions grouped together in each of the two published collections, *Cross Channel* and *The Lemon Table*, recall the individual chapters of *A History of the World in 10¹/₂ Chapters* in the sense they all seem to function autonomously as individual pieces of fiction while also interconnecting in a number of ways. They differ interestingly in mode, structure, tone, and narrative technique, but common themes, motifs, and symbols link them. Barnes has insisted, however, that *A History of the World in 10¹/₂ Chapters* should be classified as a novel, since 'it was conceived as a whole and executed as a whole' (Cook L10); he has not made this claim about *Cross Channel* or *The Lemon Table*.

The overarching theme of *Cross Channel*, suggested by the title itself, is the various experiences of British and Irish people in France at a number of different points in history. The ten pieces (as Adrian

Kempton says, 'it would be misleading to refer to them all as short stories' [95]) are not arranged chronologically. The volume moves from the early twentieth century, with 'Interference', a story about a monstrously arrogant British composer's isolated final years in France, back to the mid nineteenth century, with 'Junction', which narrates the building of a railway line by British navvies between Paris and Rouen, and then ahead to the late twentieth century with 'Experiment', in which the narrator recounts his uncle Freddy's tale of having participated, during a visit to France in the 1920s, in a sexual experiment designed by the surrealists. The elegiac 'Evermore' is concerned with the need of its elderly protagonist to visit the cemeteries in France where those, such as her brother, who died in the Great War are buried. The story focuses on her fear that the graveyards will be ploughed up and that the names of those who sacrificed their lives will not live 'FOR EVERMORE', as some of their headstones proclaim (94). 'Evermore', says Barnes, 'is about the fear that things will be forgotten, but of course history will be forgotten just as people will be forgotten' (Guignery 'History' 69). Against all odds, though, the short fictions in *Cross Channel* make their bids for remembrance, inasmuch as they bring the past to our attention.

The topics that unify the 11 short fictions of *The Lemon Table* are aging and death, and, as was also true of *Cross Channel*, the title encapsulates the dominant theme. It is not until the last story, 'The Silence', though, that we learn the title's meaning. There, the narrator, an elderly composer based on Jean Sibelius, tells us that he sometimes dines with friends at 'the lemon table', at which 'it is permissible—indeed, obligatory—to talk about death'. The enigmatic name of this society, we are told, originated in China, where 'the lemon is the symbol of death' (233). On the whole, the characters of *The Lemon Table* do not view the discomforts of aging and the prospect of death with calm acceptance. '[I]t is noticeable', observes Caroline Moore, 'that there is little here of mellowness, warmth, or even resignation (unless one counts moods of drained melancholy)' ('How to Pass' 1). Barnes, who is well aware of the volume's bleakness, says that

> [i]ts hidden subtitle is, 'Against Serenity,' because I never believed that old age was a condition in which most people come to peace with themselves and the rest of the world. I think that most people's experience

is that the heart and the emotions continue long, often embarrassingly long, after they're expected to . . . . *The Lemon Table* is about the last strugglings and flailings of the emotional life as the end nears. (McCloskey 1)

As the author of numerous books that are inventive, diverse, and rich in their intellectual and emotional appeal, Julian Barnes has had a highly distinguished career up to the present time. His achievements have been recognized in the form of the many literary awards that he has won. I have already mentioned the Somerset Maugham Award, the Booker Prize nominations, the Geoffrey Faber Memorial Prize, and the *Prix Médicis*. In France, he has also been awarded the Gutenberg Prize and the *Prix Fémina*, and he was recently made a *Commandeur de l'Ordre des Arts et des Lettres*. He has received the *Premio Grinzane Cavour* in Italy, the Shakespeare Prize in Germany, and the E. M. Forster Award in the United States. On the evidence of his most recent work, *Arthur & George*, he has lost none of his imaginative power. His best might well be yet to come.

PART II
Major Works

3

METROLAND AND *ARTHUR & GEORGE*

IDENTITY FORMATION

Pairing Barnes's first novel and his most recent one as a way of beginning my detailed analysis of his fiction might seem capricious. Set in the 1960s and 1970s and narrated in the first-person, *Metroland* is, at least in part, autobiographical; it draws upon Barnes's adolescent experience of commuting on the Metropolitan Line from the suburbs to the City of London School. The Man Booker Prize–nominated *Arthur & George*, in contrast, is a historical novel based on the real-life involvement of Sir Arthur Conan Doyle in the case of the solicitor George Edalji, the son of an Indian father and English mother, who in 1903 was wrongfully convicted and imprisoned for maiming farm animals. The novel features an undramatized third-person narrator and combines the conventions of biography, courtroom drama, and detective story. It mimics the leisurely pace, sober tone, and formal prose style of much early twentieth-century fiction (even the cover art provided by Jonathan Cape is faux-Edwardian), whereas *Metroland*, a sprightlier, briefer affair altogether, is memorable for the whimsicality, epigrammatic wit, and scathing irony of its youthful protagonist, Christopher Lloyd. His glib, withering scrutiny of societal institutions and mores—as well as of his own behaviour, motives, and beliefs— amounts almost to a general scepticism about the very foundation of things. Because as narrator Chris is responsible for the novel's 'voice' and characteristic tone, he imparts to the very narrative texture of *Metroland* a self-deflating, postmodernist quality that is missing in *Arthur & George*. Its realism is less troubled, grounded as it is in the period detail and archival documents that Barnes uses to achieve what Henry James called 'solidity of specification' (35).

Both novels, however, are *Bildungsromane*. Both depict the formative experiences of their protagonists, probe the underpinnings of their identities, and chart the evolution of those identities into adulthood. The conception of subjectivity that emerges from this treatment in both *Metroland* and *Arthur & George* is, in some respects, compatible with much recent thinking on identity in critical theory. Many French theorists, such as Louis Althusser, Jacques Lacan, and Michel Foucault, have rejected the liberal humanist belief in the unity, rationality, and agency of the individual. Indeed, as Andrew Bennet and Nicholas Royle point out, theorists today tend to prefer the term 'subject' to 'individual':

> [T]he term 'individual' (etymologically from the Latin *individuus*, 'undivided' or 'not divisible'), misleadingly suggests a sense of the 'I'as simply free, as being one with itself. . . . The usefulness of the term 'subject' . . . is that it encourages a more critical attentiveness to the fact that the 'I' is *not* autonomous. . . . Rather an 'I' or 'me' is always *subject* to forces and effects both outside itself (environmental, social, cultural, economic, educational, etc.) and 'within' itself (in particular in terms of what is called the unconscious or, in more recent philosophical terms, otherness). (104–5)

In both *Metroland* and *Arthur & George*, Barnes suggests that the forces both without and within that at once constitute and constrain the subject are inextricably linked, for in large measure the personal identities of the protagonists are formed in and from the cultural environment in which they are situated. Biological factors, such as George Edalji's myopia and dark skin pigmentation, certainly play a role, but more important in the formation of his personality is the way in which these physical traits are coded in his turn-of-the-twentieth-century society. Nature, in other words, is a blank page on which culture writes. Rather than inhering in the subject and defining it in some essential fashion, a sense of identity results from the internalization of narratives and images that circulate in families, local communities, and societies at large. The subject will try to harmonize those representations psychologically, but, as Catherine Belsey argues, they may be fundamentally in conflict: ' "Identity," subjectivity, is . . . a matrix of subject-positions, which may be inconsistent or even in contradiction with one another' (61). The representations that form the subject's sense of self have ideological effects since they either buttress or undermine existing power structures. The representations derive from many sources, religion being a prominent one, and, at least implicitly, they offer explanations, justifications, or critiques of why a given society is structured as it is. Thus, as Barnes shows in both novels, the narratives that provide the identities of his main characters prominently display the categories—such as gender, class, nationality, and race—that are used to classify and control groups of people.

In *Metroland* and *Arthur & George*, Barnes thematizes two other ideas about subjectivity that are commonplace in contemporary theory: the notion that the cultural environment in which the subject is formed is largely that of language and the corollary that the most basic force to which the 'I' is subject is language.[1] Children do not come to language as fully formed, conscious individuals, but rather language is the ground in which their identities are fashioned and in which they become conscious of themselves as individuals. The various snippets of narratives within which people come to recognize themselves render their identities textual. As Donald Hall states succinctly, 'in exploring subjectivity, we are in effect exploring the "self" as a text, as a topic for critical analysis, both in and beyond its relationship to the traditional texts of literature and culture' (5). Much has been written in the poststructuralist tradition about the fissured, decentred character of both subjectivity and other kinds of texts. Barnes's novels are in accord with this thinking in showing that personal identity is severed from any authenticating, enduring reality outside of the ephemeral, sometimes contradictory, social forces played out in language. And of course Barnes's texts themselves can be seen to be just as lacking in a solid foundation as the identities of his characters. I have said that *Arthur & George* seems to be anchored realistically by its apparent historical weight, but by implication it is just as adrift ontologically as the more self-consciously artificial *Metroland*.

METROLAND

In a circular, albeit somewhat fragmentary, fashion, the tripartite *Metroland* charts the process by which the adolescent Chris Lloyd prepares to break away from the middle-class home of his parents only to return as an adult, after a brief sojourn in Paris, to the very suburban way of life that he had seemed to repudiate. The novel raises, without answering unambiguously, the question of whether this return should be viewed as a betrayal of the youthful ideals that he had formed in partnership with his friend Toni Barbarowski or a mature acceptance of the ordinary satisfactions, sacrifices, and compromises that are a part of middle-class living. Barnes has complained that in reviewing the novel Bernard Levin missed the ambiguity of its conclusion in his claim that *Metroland* is a celebration of the values of suburbia (Freiburg 62; Levin 42), but in his analysis of the novel Matthew Pateman seems to take the opposite, equally untenable, position that Barnes's perspective on Chris's return to Metroland is predominantly ironic and disapproving (*Julian Barnes* 4–12).

The ineradicable ambiguity of the ending stems partly from, in the terminology of Mikhail Bakhtin, the novel's dialogism or polyphony. Evident not only in *Metroland* but in all of Barnes's fictions, it is largely responsible for their anti-foundational character. In contrast to monologic works, which are dominated by a single perspective or worldview, dialogic works feature multiple voices and stylistic registers that are not subordinated to an overriding authority. Dialogism is achieved not only through the sometimes conflicting points of view of a given novel's characters and narrator; it emerges also from the use of what Bakhtin called doubly voiced discourse, which he defined as writing that 'is directed both toward the referential object of speech, as in ordinary discourse, and toward *another's discourse*, toward *someone else's speech*' (*Problems* 185).

Metroland is dialogic in featuring not one but several stylistic registers, which range from the formal to the highly informal, and in featuring doubly voiced discourse in the form of parodic remarks and quotations from and allusions to the writings of others. Dialogism is particularly noticeable in the third part, which dramatizes an extensive debate between Chris and Toni, who has kept alive in himself the spirit of rebellion that has died in Chris. Toni criticizes nearly every aspect of Chris's increasingly bourgeois pattern of life, including his marriage and his career in advertising. Chris defends himself vigorously against Toni's attacks, but, because the dialogic approach relativizes the novel's point of view, readers are offered no firm basis for siding clearly with either of the characters. Toni's charge that Chris is now pursuing goals that they formerly scorned is undeniably just, but Chris's defence that he has not so much sold out as grown up also has a certain persuasiveness. In contrast to Chris, Toni does seem rather immature in his uncompromising, angry attitudes. As Pateman observes, Toni's authority is vitiated by the insensitive, reductive nature of both his views and personality (*Julian Barnes* 10).

Barnes's narrative technique adds to *Metroland*'s ambiguity by sending the irony in two directions at once. As I have already mentioned, irony is immediately noticeable in the tone of voice of the adolescent Chris, who explains that his and Toni's 'coruscating idealism expressed itself naturally in a public pose of raucous cynicism' (15). Because of the retrospective nature of Chris's narration, however, the irony sometimes seems to be directed against the extreme, overly simplistic views that he and Toni hold on various social issues. Merritt Moseley notices that the adult Chris, who is looking back on his teenage years, 'is now capable of ironic correction of the ideas and postures of his adolescent self. The first-person narration combines an inhabiting of the mind of an adolescent with an older man's understanding of that mind's shortcomings' (19). At any given moment, readers can be either listening to the older man interpret and judge his younger self or experiencing the teenager's consciousness without this mediation. This narrative method generates irony that undermines the positions of both the adolescent and the adult. What makes the irony doubly directed is the fact that the younger Chris's comments point ahead in judgement at the very bourgeois way of life that his older self has adopted, just as the older Chris's comments point backward critically at the naivety of his younger self. Each saws away at the branch upon which the other is sitting. Neither of the two perspectives carries more weight than the other. The adult Chris's views are not more authoritative than those of his adolescent self by dint of his greater life experience, since they seem as much a product of complacency as of maturity and wisdom. He tries to justify abandoning his youthful ideals by challenging the reader with a witty rhetorical question: '[I]sn't part of growing up being able to ride irony without being thrown?' (135). But overtly recognizing the irony inherent in the transformation that he has undergone as an adult does not make him any less an apostate.

Although in *Metroland* Barnes does not show the development of his protagonist's identity from its beginnings in early childhood, as he does with Arthur and George in his most recent novel, in Part One he does dramatize the importance of adolescent peer groups in the shaping of subjectivity. Chris and Toni are extremely close friends who have formed their own subculture in opposition to the dominant, middle-class one of their parents and teachers. (Toni's situation is different from Chris's in that his parents, Jewish refugees from Poland, are not typically English, but the two boys seem equally alienated from their families.) Because they are intellectually inclined students at an academically superior school, the duo's identification of themselves as rebels originates not in the models available to them in the mass culture of movies and popular music but in their study of French literature and language. Barnes's first novel, which incorporates many untranslated phrases and sentences in French, introduced readers to what would become a recurrent area of interest in his fiction and non-fiction: the places, history, culture, and customs of France. For Chris and Toni, as Moseley states, 'France is an idea, as well as a style, a language, a pose, an image of the right sort of life, and a rebuke to Metroland' (30).

What attracts the boys about French literature is the combativeness of many of its writers, whom Chris dubs 'sophisticated toughs' (16), and their elevation of art as an ideal worth living for. Chris's and Toni's admiration for these authors fuels their own opposition to the suburban values of their elders, and it also takes them in the direction of aestheticism. Although they respect twentieth-century writers (especially those such as Albert Camus, who were also capable athletes), they have a special love for Gustave Flaubert, Charles Baudelaire, and the Symbolist poets (two of the novels epigraphs are taken from Arthur Rimbaud and Paul Verlaine). Priding themselves on being deracinated (32), Chris and Toni sink imaginative roots into the worlds of literature and painting, worshipping 'the purity of the language, the perfectibility of the self, the function of art, plus a clutch of capitalized intangibles like Love, Truth, Authenticity' (15). The boys have an innocent belief in the morally improving power of art that was lacking in their nineteenth-century heroes, whose pursuit of *l'art pour l'art* was, in effect, a rejection of didacticism (29). Moseley is right to say that Chris's and Toni's aestheticism is essentially apolitical (23), a fact that becomes explicit in the novel's third part when the adult Toni, now a committed leftist, criticizes their youthful indifference to politics as passive support for the Tories (145).

The place of France in the lives of Chris and Toni demonstrates how central the concept of nation can be in the ongoing process of self-fashioning. The pair set up a dichotomy whereby France stands metonymically for traits and experiences that they see as desirable, such as freedom, exoticism, glamour, artistic richness, sexual excitement, and social non-conformity, and England stands for staidness, blinkered traditionalism, unreflective habit, philistine indifference to aesthetic values, and oppressive adult authority. The fact that their understanding of France is flawed by ignorance and immature thinking and that their view of their own country is inconsistent does not mean that their ideas about the two nations are any less potent in helping to shape their individual identities. I have said that England usually functions negatively as a metonymy for the elements in their social and psychological environments that they perceive as retarding their self development, but central London sometimes represents and contains for them a desired urban sophistication and cosmopolitanism: 'London, we read somewhere, combined everything you could require' (27). Consequently, despite the absence of *quais* and *boulevards*, they are able to conflate London with nineteenth-century Paris in the fantasies which they enact of being *flâneurs* (17).

The processes of identity formation that we witness in the teenaged Chris demonstrate the role of social class and also illustrate Belsey's point, which I quoted earlier, that the subject positions which collectively constitute an individual's sense of self are often contradictory. As remorseless critics of the bourgeoisie, Chris and Toni believe that they conform to middle-class conventions only grudgingly, out of necessity as adolescents who are dependent upon their parents. They pride themselves upon the acts of rudeness that they perpetrate as part of their program, derived from their French models, to outrage some of the respectable adults whom they encounter (*épater la bourgeoisie* [Barnes *Metroland* 15]). Yet Chris seems unaware that certain experiences that he is delighted to have undergone because they enhance his sense of self-worth are, in fact, rites of passage into adulthood in the middle class. For example, the first time that he is called 'sir' by a lower-middle-class clerk in a clothing store is an occasion for joy, clearly because it confirms his superior position in the social hierarchy: 'I could have fainted; I could, at the very least, have grinned. Instead I just stood, helpless with happiness, while Mr Foster knelt at my feet and piled on the praise' (20). Chris mockingly labels the men travelling to work on the train with him as the 'pinstripes and the chalkstripes' (59), but he is proud to carry a rolled umbrella because it confers social status (19), and his own daydreams of attaining adulthood feature him 'owning cufflinks, collar studs and monogrammed handkerchiefs' (62). A suit, pinstriped or chalk-striped, presumably, will be required to give these accessories a function.

Chris's imagined rebellion against the values of his class does not result in any identification with or sympathy for the lower classes. Rather, they are for him the potentially dangerous Other who confirm his unacknowledged solidarity with the social class in which he has been brought up. His regular sight of the slums of Kilburn from his Metropolitan Line train inspires thoughts of 'the pullulating mass of the working class, who at any moment might swarm like termites up the viaduct and take the pinstripes apart' (60–1). We are not far here from Matthew Arnold's spectre of social anarchy, but, unlike Arnold, Chris has very little concern for the well being of the working class, whom he pejoratively compares to termites. Rather than proposing the extension of culture to the poor as a way to enrich their lives and prevent anarchy, he uses their blighted living conditions as grist for his own private aesthetic mill. He likens what he can see to Gustave Doré's nineteenth-century drawings of squalid London scenes (60), and he is proud to be able to show Toni the view of Kilburn and other slums from his train. All of the sights are 'relevant, fulfilling, sensibility sharpening. And what was life about if not that?' (61). It is hard to see how his callous attitude to the privations endured by others supports his earlier claim about the civilizing, morally improving power of art.

In depicting the evolution of Chris's subjectivity, Barnes deals overtly with the instrumental role of language in the process. He shows, for example, how adolescent peer groups create their own argot in order to solidify a sense of collective identity. The boys at Chris's school devise their own slang, fix as a group upon swear words of choice (the euphemism 'fug' is favoured by Chris and Toni), and use language ritualistically. 'RooooOOOOOOOOOiiiiined', Chris informs us, 'was the school cry, drawn out and modulated in the way we imagined hyenas to howl. Gilchrist did the screechiest, most fearing version; Leigh one with a breaking sob in the middle of the vowel howl; but everyone did it at least adequately' (21).

Barnes goes beyond suggesting that individuals and groups use language purposefully in fashioning their identities. More disconcertingly he insists that language determines the nature of the self that is fashioned. Living in Paris and speaking French exclusively, Chris finds to his chagrin that the language has endowed him with personality traits that conflict with those that he exhibited when speaking his native language:

> I definitely became aware, if not of saying things I didn't believe, at least of saying things I didn't know I'd thought in ways I hadn't previously considered. I found myself more prone to generalisation, to labelling and ticketing and docketing. . . . I felt, too, as if one part of me was being faintly disloyal to another part. (106)

Barnes has confessed to the autobiographical nature of this experience, saying of his own year in France that by the end 'I wasn't really recognizing myself as the same person' because 'the language influences the thoughts you can have' (McGrath 23).

In the same interview, Barnes says that he finds the general proposition that language constitutes our reality 'quite attractive' (23), and in *Metroland* he shows how destabilizing in an ontological sense such a recognition can be. The occasion for this disclosure is Chris's failure to prevent his Parisian lover, Annick, from leaving him by telling her unequivocally that he loves her. After she has departed, Chris speculates about his own rather uncertain and shifting feelings about her in relation to the signifier 'love'. His premises, reasoning, and conclusions seem perfectly deconstructionist in tenor:

> Well, what about the simple question . . . do I love her? Depends on what you mean by love. When do you cross the dividing line? When does *je t' aime bien* become *je t' aime?* The easy answer is, you know when you're in love, because there's no way you can doubt it, any more than you can doubt it when your house is on fire. That's the trouble, though: try to describe the phenomenon and you get either a tautology or a metaphor. . . . Hesitancy doesn't indicate lack of feeling, just uncertainty about terminology . . . Doesn't the terminology affect the emotion in any case? Shouldn't I just have said *je t'aime* (and who's to say I wouldn't have been telling the truth)? Naming can lead to making. (125)

Chris's scepticism here about the existence of an emotional reality outside the dynamics of language is especially significant when we remember the place of love in his value system and self-image. Love had been one of the ideals venerated in the abstract by him and Toni in their adolescence, and, just before becoming sexually intimate with Annick, he had seemed ready to grasp that now-embodied ideal, even as other aspects of his identity seemed to be coalescing in Paris:

> It felt as if everything was coming together, all at once. The past was all around; I was the present; art was here, and history, and now the promise of something much like love or sex. . . . And bringing it all together, ingesting it, making it mine, was me—fusing all the art and the history with what I might soon, with luck, be calling the life. (93)

In losing Annick and deconstructing love, therefore, what Chris is doing is dislodging one of the foundations of his own identity.

Scepticism about the nature of love is also evident in what Chris narrates about his marriage to Marion. He is attracted by her apparent honesty, as he had been by Annick's, but he discovers that her respect for truth leads her to submit ideals to a withering scrutiny. She holds that self-interest, and not undying, ennobling passion, is the motivation for most marriages (116), and, while she does not dismiss the reality of love entirely, she certainly sees it as an indefinable, mutable, contingent phenomenon. Her answer to Chris's question 'Will you love me regardless of what happens?' is a blunt 'You must be off your head' (141). Her confession to him that on one occasion during their marriage she had had sex with another man introduces the recurrent theme in Barnes's *oeuvre* of sexual infidelity. She confidently predicts that he, too, will be unfaithful. 'It's too interesting not to', she tells him (162).

Art, another primary support for Chris's sense of self as an adolescent, proves no more durable in this regard than love. It is no exaggeration to say that art had become a surrogate religion for him, helping to assuage the fear of death that had overcome him in the wake of his rejection of Christianity and the concept of God (54–5). But his belief in the ancient claim for art's immortality cannot survive his learning at school about 'the concept of planet death' (55). According to science, at some point in the future the earth and everything on it—including the paintings in the National Gallery that Chris loves to visit, the plays of Shakespeare, and the novels of Flaubert—will be destroyed in a final, gigantic conflagration. Of course, art continues after this point to have meaning for Chris, and, as Peter Childs says, art is an important theme in all of Barnes's fictions precisely because 'its intellectual value lies in its attempt to make sense of the world' (86). In the absence of absolutes, however, the status of that sense-making is very much in doubt. In his conversation with Toni near the novel's end, Chris confesses that he believes that the significance of art is always only subjective at best and illusory at worst. Like the existence of God, the value of art depends upon faith, and, he tells Toni, 'for the moment I've lapsed' (167). Moreover, as Childs points out, even when art does seem significant, that significance might seem distant from lives of those who intuit the significance: 'the idea that art is the most important thing "in life" is partly paradoxical because in Barnes's books art and life are often contrasted' (86). It is not just that (in the words from Auden's poem on Yeats quoted by Chris) '*poetry* makes nothing happen' (145); it is that the gap between art and life might be insurmountable. Even in their youth, says Chris, he and Toni feared 'that our passion for art was the result of the emptiness of our "lives"' (128).

It is always possible, of course, for readers to deflect the implicit challenge to the solidity of their own identities represented by Chris's situation: they could dismiss him as a sellout who lacks their own integrity, as Toni does (166). Rather than viewing Chris's case as a general statement by Barnes about the vacuity of individual identity, we could read him as a negative exemplum, someone who could have avoided his fate had he had the courage of his convictions. In other words, we could conclude that Barnes wants us to reject Chris, not to identify with him. Moseley likens him to Joyce's Stephen Dedalus (18), but rather than seeing Chris as a semi-autobiographical version of Barnes himself in his development as a novelist, we could view *Metroland* as a wholly ironic *Portrait of the Artist Manqué*. Whereas Joyce's Stephen is a real artist-in-the-making, who remains alienated from his society, Barnes's Chris is a poseur, who only dabbles while in Paris at being a writer and who allows himself to be re-integrated into the bourgeoisie. To complete this interpretation, we could note that Chris becomes not a distinguished writer of serious fiction but first an advertiser and later an editor of superficial coffee-table books. The problem, however, with a reading that creates too much ironic distance between Barnes and us on the one hand and Chris on the other is that it overlooks the ambiguity that I discussed earlier. Concluding that Barnes totally repudiates Chris necessitates ignoring qualities that make him a sympathetic figure: his humane intelligence, his urbane sophistication and wit, his devotion to his family, and his struggle to be a decent, honest person. If we miss the ambiguity of *Metroland*'s denouement, we fail to read carefully enough.

ARTHUR & GEORGE

The dialogic nature of *Arthur & George* is readily apparent in its division into sections, almost all of which are titled either 'Arthur' or 'George', that establish the book as 'a pair of alternating biographies, a tale of opposites' (Adams 25). The novel swings, in pendulum-like fashion, between the points of view of Arthur Conan Doyle and George Edalji, who could not be more different in personality, motivation, appearance, and capabilities. Their beliefs and perspectives on the world frequently clash, but despite the obvious limitations of both characters, Barnes's undramatized third-person narrator does not correct their misperceptions and prejudices in order to provide readers with a broader understanding of reality. The prominent theme in this novel of clear vision (in both the literal and metaphoric senses) proves highly paradoxical, for Barnes shows the impossibility of achieving Arnold's goal of '[seeing] life steadily, and [seeing] it whole' ('To a Friend' 2). The narrator is omniscient in a psychological sense in having complete access to his protagonists' inner lives, but he maintains a Flaubertian detachment. The novel contains many passages written in free indirect style, which combine features of the characters' direct speech with those of the narrator's indirect reports, but the narrator refuses to pronounce authoritatively on matters that are in dispute, to offer moral judgements, or to clear up all of the novel's mysteries and uncertainties. *Arthur & George*'s dialogism is deepened with the addition of other voices, such as those of Arthur's sister Connie, who contests Arthur's spiritualist views, and the policeman Captain Anson, who engages in a lengthy dispute with Arthur about the Edalji case. As Jon Barnes observes, 'the story unspools in a variety of voices and points of view, all jostling for narrative pre-eminence, bickering among themselves about the truth' (19).

The historical context for this collision of beliefs and opinions is an Edwardian society that is, beneath its seemingly confident surface, troubled and anxious. Caroline Moore is right to say that the novel 'is partly about the pain and uncertainty that comes with the crumbling of old certainties (belief in orthodox religion, in the Empire, in codes of sexual honour and the impartiality of British justice)' ('Far from Elementary' 1). The religious aspect of this crisis is reflected in the lives of Arthur and George, both of whom lose faith in the Christianity of their parents. Barnes gives readers a strong sense of the violence and disorder that threaten the ostensible solidity of a nation teetering on the brink of the twentieth-century's turbulence and chaos. The senseless savagery of the Great Wyrley Outrages and the relentless racist scapegoating of the obviously innocent George in recrimination for them are the novel's expression of the cruel energies that underlie English society's civilized surface. As Peter Kemp states, *Arthur & George* is like many Edwardian novels in depicting 'close-to-home savagery behind the imperial façade, and unruly impulses festering beneath the veneer of decorum' (38).

The cultural gap between *Arthur & George*'s turn-of-the-twentieth-century characters and Barnes's twenty-first-century readers allows us to see that history is perhaps the most powerful shaper of identity. It does not completely determine the forms of subjectivity, any more than genetics does (if such were the case, then how could we account for people who are out of step with the cultural norms of the period in which they live?), but history does appear to open up certain possibilities of development for individuals and close off others. Both Arthur and George exhibit psychological character-istics and betray attitudes—about sexual morality, for example—that seem typical of late Victorian society. Barnes shows how the two men respond to its rigid expectations about the relationship between gender and personal identity. Arthur is completely suc-cessful in attaining the social ideal of manliness, with his aggressive, forthright demeanour, athletic prowess, and love of dangerous out-door activities. In contrast, the sexually and socially timid George, short-sighted, bookish, and unskilled at sports, fails totally to meet the standard of masculinity. It is no surprise that the well-adjusted Arthur, whose place of unrivalled authority as his family's patriarch depends upon the continuation of existing gender roles, opposes the movement for women's rights (163), while George, the life-long bachelor whose only intimate friend is his sister, is ahead of his time in championing equality for the sexes (330).

Arthur & George depicts how the extreme separation of the sexes in Edwardian England in education and other areas of life made men more ignorant of women than they otherwise would be. Arthur is fully conscious that this segregation denied him familiarity with the details of their lives, but he thinks this a good thing: '[h]e is solidly content with the separation and distinction of the sexes as devel-oped by society in its wisdom through the centuries.... Knowing women less he is able to idealize them more. This is as he thinks it should be' (163). But such ignorance does not always lead to chival-rous notions about women's purity and goodness, as it does in

Arthur's case. In *Metroland* it leads Chris to denigrate girls rather than to glorify them. Though the sexes were not nearly so separate in the late 1950s and early 1960s, Chris does attend an all-boys school. As a teenager he goes through a stage of contempt for young women that, like his propensity to objectify them rather crudely in physical terms, seems largely a reaction to sexual fear. He tells us that his first evening with Ginny, his brother's first girl friend, was spent 'hating her . . . for being herself. A girl, a different order of being' (64).

As he does in *Metroland*, in *Arthur & George* Barnes displays the ways in which individual identity converges with ideas about collective, national identity. In fact, one reviewer calls the novel 'a sort of parable of English identity' (Tait 26). Both of Barnes's protagonists identify fully with the grandeur and might of England, then at the height of world domination. When George is a small boy, every night his father makes him recite the catechism that their Staffordshire vicarage is at the very centre of England, 'the beating heart of the Empire', and that 'the blood that flows through the arteries and veins of the Empire to reach even its farthest shore' is the Anglican Church (17). Of young Arthur, Barnes tells us that 'English history inspired him; English freedoms made him proud; English cricket made him patriotic. And the greatest epoch in English history was the fourteenth century. . . . For Arthur the root of Englishness lay in the long-gone, long-remembered world of chivalry' (23).

Owing to complications in their lineage, however, neither of Barnes's protagonists is allowed to feel naturally and fully English. Arthur's situation sensitizes him to the fact that national identity is a social construction, not a natural phenomenon. Consequently, it can be acquired by those for whom it is not simply a birthright: 'Irish by ancestry, Scottish by birth, instructed in the faith of Rome by Dutch Jesuits, Arthur became English' (23). So successful in this regard does the creator of the Holmes stories become that in his various roles he seems to personify the best of England: 'Knight of the realm, friend of the King, champion of the Empire, and Deputy Lieutenant of Surrey', he was a 'man constantly in public demand' (197). For all that he wins the adulation of his countrymen, Arthur is aware of a gap between his outward identity and the depths of his psyche, where, to some degree, he still feels himself to be an outsider. 'In some ways,' says the narrator, 'he has always felt a fraud, and the more famous he has become, the more fraudulent he has felt' (203). Barnes's Doyle, one imagines, would be able to empathize with another renowned writer, Robert Graves, when he says of his own name, 'I am not he/either in mind or limb' (107). Upon meeting George, Arthur tells him that he considers them both 'unofficial Englishmen' (217).

George is the opposite of Arthur in the sense that, inwardly, he feels fully English. Taken aback by Arthur's remark, he reflects: 'How is he less than a full Englishman? He is one by birth, by citizenship, by education, by religion, by profession' (217). But, because George's Indian heritage is evident in his physical appearance, his fellow citizens seldom treat him as fully English. His facial features and dark skin colour are a much more difficult barrier for him to surmount than Arthur's Irish and Scottish backgrounds are for him. One of George's earliest experiences at school is being told by a classmate, 'You're not a right sort' (9). Racial theories abounded throughout the West during the period in which the novel is set, and George is frequently stereotyped in ways that Edward Said critiqued in *Orientalism*. He states that the Orient was one of Europe's 'deepest and most recurring images of the Other', which 'has helped to define Europe . . . as its contrasting image, idea, personality, experience' (1–2). It is easy to see how characterizations of George by English officials and the newspapers serve the function of branding him an essentially foreign menace to civilized English society. For example, after George's arrest, a newspaper account of his appearance in court reads as follows:

> [T]here was little of the typical solicitor in his swarthy face, with its full, dark eyes, prominent mouth, and small round chin. His appearance is essentially Oriental in its stolidity, no sign of emotion escaping from him beyond a faint smile as the extraordinary story of the prosecution unfolded. (113–14)

What is strongly being implied here is that George is a sinister, treacherous Oriental, one who can take cold-blooded, sadistic pleasure in remembering the butchery that he inflicted on helpless farm animals.

Because Barnes tracks the lives of Arthur and George right from their early childhood, readers can see the formative power of the social discourses that are the raw material for their subjectivities. The novel shows us how both boys assimilate rules, formulate ideals, and undergo experiences that confer ways of making sense of life and coping with its difficulties. Partly through the instruction of parents, teachers, and other adults, both of them learn very early on that some narratives, such as those in the Bible, are more important and authoritative than others. Lacking imagination, indoctrinated by a stern parent who is also a clergyman, George believes in the literal truth of the Bible's precepts and stories, although when interpretation is necessary (as with Christ's parables), he is at sea (16). His religious training underpins some of his most persistent character traits, such as the commitment to honesty and truth that motivates much of his behaviour over the course of his life:

> 'I am the way, the truth and the life': he is to hear this many times on his father's lips. The way, the truth and the life. You go on your way through life telling the truth. George knows that this is not exactly what the Bible means, but as he grows up this is how the words sound to him. (4)

In Arthur's case, Christianity is a less authoritative discourse than the stories told to him by his beloved 'Mam', which link his family's genealogy with chivalric romances and make him identify fully with his namesake, King Arthur, in particular and the figure of the knight in general. His early exposure to his mother's story-telling instils in Arthur the narrative skills that eventually make him a professional writer.

Arthur is a character whose biography shows especially clearly that subjectivity is constituted by narratives, stories that individuals tell themselves to generate a coherent sense of personal identity, to answer the question 'who am I?'. Being fully conscious as a boy that his life is a romance in which he is the heroic replacement for his weak father and in which the Mam is the damsel in distress, he is focused on the problem of how to conduct his life so as to get from its beginning to its destined end: 'He would write stories: he would rescue her by describing the fictional rescue of others. These descriptions would bring him money, and money would do the rest' (24). When as an adult he attains his goal by writing the Holmes stories, he follows the same method that he uses with the plot of his own life: he conceives of the endings first and devises the other parts of the narratives so as to allow him to arrive (via Holmes's deductions) at those endings.[2]

Even though Arthur succeeds in enacting the script that he has formulated for his life, he finds when he reaches the end of the story that it does not actually correspond with the end of his life. By the time he is middle-aged, he is famous and prosperous, with a family that he loves, and a mother who is very well taken care of. The chivalric quest is complete, but 'Arthur [is] not ready for the end of his own story. . . . What [does] a knight errant do when he [comes] home to a wife and two children in South Norwood' (55)? He does find other challenges, such as serving in the Boer War and involving himself in George's case. But Arthur's biggest difficulty is in incorporating his own eventual physical death into a narrative with a happy ending, or even one with no ending at all.

Death is a reality that obsesses Arthur from his boyhood onward (his earliest memory is of seeing the corpse of his grandmother in a darkened bedroom [3]).[3] Once his Catholic faith has waned, he is unable to see his life as a providential journey to a celestial home with God. Unlike Chris in *Metroland* after he becomes an atheist, however, Arthur continues to seek a metaphysical solution to the problem of death. Like many people of his era, he believes that spiritualism (his preferred term is 'spiritism') offers an answer that can be verified empirically. There is a widespread belief that the historical Arthur Conan Doyle was credulous in accepting the claims of mediums, but Barnes's Arthur is fully aware that chicanery is frequently employed at séances. Nevertheless, based on the evidence of his own senses and the testimony of certain renowned scientists, he believes that the spirits of the dead actually do sometimes speak to the living. Life, therefore, must continue on after physical death.

Because *Arthur & George* is so thoroughly dialogized, however, its readers are not invited to accept Arthur's point of view on spiritualism as authoritative. Sceptics, such as his sister Connie and George, critique and counterbalance Arthur's views. After his death, does his spirit, as some claim, appear at the memorial service held for him in London's Albert Hall? What does George, who is in attendance, see as he gazes with binoculars at the empty chair that has been placed on the stage for Arthur to sit in? If the spirit does survive the death of the body, can it be seen only through the lens of faith? Should we think of the narrative of Arthur's life as continuing on as a comedy, or has it been a tragedy that terminated once and for all with his death? For answers, we have only George's inconclusive thoughts: 'He does not know whether he has seen truth or lies, or a mixture of both. He does not know if the clear, surprising, unEnglish fervour of those around him this evening is proof of charlatanry or belief. And if belief, whether true or false' (356).

However unwavering his belief in the afterlife might be, Arthur, like Chris in *Metroland*, has moments of crisis during which he doubts the truth of the narratives that sustain his sense of identity. Like the teenaged Chris, Arthur, whose imagination has been nurtured in tales of chivalry, idealizes love, which ennobles his life. In his view, the very meaning of his life is inseparable from the loving relationships that he has established, first with his first wife, Touie, and then with Jean Leckie, who becomes his second wife after Touie's death. But what is the status of that love in relation to reality? Does it have an enduring existence, or is it simply one of the mutable emotions that daily course through his breast? And most crucially for the scientifically minded Arthur, how can the actuality of love be proved? 'When the fit is on me', he confides to his mother,

> I doubt everything. I doubt I ever loved Touie. I doubt I love my children. I doubt my literary capability. I doubt Jean loves me.... I think it, I believe it, but how can I ever know it? If only I could prove it, if either of us could prove it. (189–90)

Arthur's difficulties here instantiate Pateman's general claim that Barnes's fiction reflects the postmodern condition, the 'perceived loss of legitimation ... accounted for by Jean-François Lyotard as resulting from the fragmentation of those narratives which used to provide a single and trustworthy explanation of our behaviour and existence' ('Popularity of Ethics' 181). No longer secure in his religious faith, Arthur cannot confidently draw on the Christian narrative to find an eternal sanction for human love in divine love. As Pateman further states, in such a confused, relativistic context, the individual becomes 'the sole arbiter of ethics' (180). This is the predicament that Arthur finds himself in when he rejects the charge of his brother-in-law, Willie Hornung, that he has flouted society's moral standards in appearing publicly with Jean while Touie is still alive. Willie holds that '[h]onour is not just a matter of internal good feeling, but also of external behaviour'; but for Arthur, personal honour is a matter of inner purity, not of outward appearance (178). He argues that, because his relationship with Jean is platonic, it is honourable. But, having conceived of honour subjectively, he confesses to his mother that he cannot readily define it or differentiate it from its opposite: 'It sometimes seems that honour and dishonour lie so close together, closer than I ever imagined' (190). We are not too far here from the nominalism of Falstaff's famous denial of the reality of honour in *King Henry IV, Part I*: 'What is honour? A word. What is in that word honour? What is that honour? Air. A trim reckoning!' (5.1.134–6).

The novel's treatment of George also reveals the ontological precariousness of the narratives out of which subjectivity is created. As a solicitor, he values the order and justice that the English legal system provides. It is no accident that he writes a book on railway law, for he sees life as a journey to the destination of justice, and the 'railway suggests how it ought to be, how it could be: a smooth ride to a terminus on evenly spaced rails and according to an agreed timetable' (50). After the ordeal of his arrest and imprisonment destroys his religious faith, the law totally replaces biblical stories and precepts as the foundation of his identity. But, cruelly and paradoxically, the very legal system on which his subjectivity rests is the vehicle for the injustice that he suffers. It is the law that nullifies the very sense of selfhood that he has fashioned from it. Because of his conviction, he is stripped of his highly valued professional identity as a solicitor, an anonymous prison number is substituted for his proper name, and 'his story [is] taken away from him' (129). His dilemma reminds us that our self-images are constructed not only from the stories that we tell ourselves about who we are but also from the stories that others tell about us. As I have said, Orientalism is the source of the damning narrative about George that the police, journalists, and prosecuting attorneys cobble together. The subtle changes that the authorities make in it as the trial proceeds should signal its falsity (123), but George is convicted nonetheless. The prosecuting counsel's account of his role in the Outrages, George realizes, is 'just a story, . . . something made up from scraps and coincidences and hypotheses; he knew, too, that he was innocent; but something about the repetition of the story by an authority in wig and gown made it take on extra plausibility' (121).

It is not merely narratives fabricated out of malice and prejudice that Barnes exposes as baseless in *Arthur & George*. The novel is by no means glibly postmodernist in its anti-foundationalism, but it is consistent with many of Barnes's other fictions in raising questions about the truth claims of social discourses. For example, the portrait of George delineated by Arthur in the document that is intended both to prove his innocence and to expose the real culprit does not so much represent George's essential self as it fragments his identity and renders it fictional: 'It made him feel like several overlapping people at the same time: a victim seeking redress; a solicitor facing the highest tribunal in the country; and a character in a novel' (297). The last statement constitutes a highly self-conscious moment in *Arthur & George*, one that momentarily violates its realism to expose the artifice behind it, for Barnes's George is, finally, a character in a novel. Arthur's description of George does not reveal him to himself; rather, it deconstructs itself in undecidability: the portrait 'was all true, and yet untrue; flattering, yet unflattering; believable, yet unbelievable' (298). George concludes that Arthur's case against Sharp—based on weak circumstantial evidence and inferences drawn to support a conclusion arrived at in advance—'strangely resembled the Staffordshire Constabulary's case against himself' (304). The faith that George continues to have in England's legal system is rewarded in an equally ambiguous way. The Government's official report exonerates him but also rejects compensation and blames him for his own misfortune. George sums up the message of the report in an aporia that recalls Arthur's designation of himself at once honourable and dishonourable: '[i]nnocent yet guilty' (316).

In frustrating the expectation that the creator of Sherlock Holmes will solve the mystery of the Great Wyrley Outrages, Barnes, as Natasha Walter puts it, 'allow[s] us to reflect on the difference between the knowability of detective fiction and the unknowability of real life' (26). *Arthur & George* is like several of Barnes's novels in its paradoxical accomplishment of dramatizing history in all of its detail and substantiality while simultaneously sensitizing us to the ephemerality and nebulousness of the past. Invoking Geoffrey

Braithwaite's striking metaphor in *Flaubert's Parrot* that compares history to a piglet smeared with grease, Jon Barnes says of Julian Barnes's accomplishment in *Arthur & George* that he 'succeeds where his fellow pig-chasers have failed, in making the most familiar materials feel unfamiliar again, palpable, surprising, real' (19). In the chapter that follows, I shall demonstrate how in *Flaubert's Parrot*, *A History of the World in 10½ Chapters*, and *England, England* Barnes splinters the potentially totalizing narratives of history, in the process casting doubt upon their claims to truth. Paradoxically, he is equally suspicious of a postmodernist readiness to dismiss those claims entirely.

4

FLAUBERT'S PARROT, A HISTORY OF THE WORLD IN 10¹/₂ CHAPTERS, AND ENGLAND, ENGLAND

REPRESENTING HISTORY

The three novels grouped together in this chapter pose and explore a variety of questions relating to history that are also frequently asked by academic theorists.[1] How do we know the past? What is the role of memory, both individual and collective, in the retrieval of history, and how trustworthy is it? Is there an independent historical reality, an untold story, behind our many historical narratives, or are those narratives invented rather than found? Can we capture the historical past accurately through empirical methods, or, as New Historicist critics such as Louis Montrose claim, is what we can know severely limited by our own embeddedness in history (29–39)? In other words, do the basic assumptions and paradigms that dominate our own historical era so totally determine what we can know that they preclude our being able to understand earlier eras objectively? If we cannot stand outside history, is real historical understanding even possible? If it is, it would seem that it is, at best, perspectival, relative, and shifting. Do the forms in which we try to represent history and the very language that we use to do it condition the nature of what is represented? Do historical patterns exist independently of our systems of signification, or are those patterns of meaning the product of those systems? To what uses do we put our representations of the past? Do our efforts feed a politically reactionary nostalgia? Do they serve cynical, mercenary ends, or, alternatively, can they help us move into the future in ways that are socially beneficial?

The topic of history overlaps with that of personal identity discussed in the previous chapter. As I mentioned in relation to *Arthur & George*, subjectivity is formed by history. Historical myths and other narratives that constitute the collective identity of a nation also help to shape the subjectivities of individuals. Consequently, *Arthur & George* says almost as much about Edwardian England as it does about the lives of its two protagonists, and the more experimental *Flaubert's Parrot*, which also draws on the genre of biography, provides detailed information about nineteenth-century France in the process of limning what Melvyn Bragg refers to as a cubist 'portrait of a writer from multiple often contending overlaid perspectives' (22). The title of *A History of the World in 10$^{1}/_{2}$ Chapters* promises a work focused as broadly as possible on history, not on the lives of one or two individuals, but Barnes's eccentric, highly selective, fractured history of the world is, in fact, narrated in episodes that centre on individual characters. *England, England*'s treatment of history is presented through the long life of its protagonist, Martha Cochrane, and especially through her involvement in Sir Jack Pitman's scheme to reduce English history to a depthless, postmodernist spectacle in the theme park that he builds on the Isle of Wight.

In the process of depicting the lives of their central characters, *Metroland* and *Arthur & George* reveal the slipperiness of language as a representational tool. The three novels discussed in this chapter go farther in making the problematics of representation their main subjects. All are metafictions that self-consciously lay bare their own artifices even as they disclose that historical narratives are less records of what happened than they are stories invented to serve a variety of human purposes, one of which (according to the narrator of 'Parenthesis') is therapy: 'We make up a story to cover the facts we don't know or can't accept; we keep a few true facts and spin a new story around them. Our panic and our pain are only eased by soothing fabulation; we call it history' (*History* 240).

It is significant that Barnes's narrator in 'Parenthesis' (who seems closely modelled on Barnes himself) does not deny the existence of facts, for this implies that the writing of history is not an entirely free activity. But what constitutes facts, which, in any case, never speak for themselves? Linda Hutcheon's distinction between 'the brute *events* of the past and the historical *facts* that we construct out of them' is relevant here. 'Facts are events to which we have given meaning' (*Politics* 57). Those meanings, dependent as they are upon interpretations, are always open to dispute, to alternative interpretations. Historical truth, therefore, lacks a hard foundation, but this does not necessarily mean that it is non-existent or that all possible interpretations are equally plausible and persuasive. Pateman is right to stress that Barnes would like to reject the extreme postmodernist view that historical narratives are fictions without any real mimetic capacity. Yet, as Pateman also says, Barnes has great difficulty in finding intellectual support for such a rejection ('Popularity of Ethics' 185–7). For example, his narrator in 'Parenthesis' says that we must either believe that some portion of objective truth is available to us or surrender the field to liars and 'admit that the victor has the right not just to the spoils but also to the truth' (*History* 244). But in the same breath he acknowledges that objective truth is only a fiction: 'We all know that objective truth is not obtainable, that when some event occurs we shall have a multiplicity of subjective truths which we assess and then fabulate into history, into some God-eyed version of what "really" happened. This God-eyed version is a fake—a charming, impossible fake' (*History* 243). As we shall see, much of the creative energy that animates *Flaubert's Parrot, A History of the World in 10½ Chapters,* and *England, England* comes from the tension between the desire for truth and the fear that it is inaccessible.

FLAUBERT'S PARROT

Short-listed in the 1984 competition for the Booker Prize, *Flaubert's Parrot* was singled out by reviewers on both sides of the Atlantic as a brilliant example of postmodernist fictional experimentation, an unclassifiably hybrid text that manages to be (in the terms of Roland Barthes) both *scriptable* or writerly and *lisible* or readerly, both intellectually challenging and highly entertaining. It was the book that established Barnes's reputation amongst readers of serious fiction as a member of the first tier of contemporary British novelists, and

more than 20 years after its appearance, it is still the accomplishment for which he is best-known. It has generated more academic
literary criticism than any of his other novels, and, along with *A History of the World in 10¹/₂ Chapters*, it is frequently singled out by critics
as Barnes's major work.[2]

Flaubert's Parrot is obsessed with the problem of loss—with the
transience of life and the perishability of people and things—
and with the question of how loss can be overcome. Narrated
by an elderly, grieving doctor, the book has an autumnal quality that is readily apparent beneath the sparkling eloquence of
both Barnes's prose and the many passages that he culls from
Flaubert's writings.[3] As Barnes has attested, Geoffrey Braithwaite's
failed attempt throughout the novel to reconstruct discursively a
stable, accurate, internally consistent representation of Flaubert's
life is motivated by (in Freudian terms) the displacement of his
emotional need to express and assuage his grief over his wife's
death (Guignery, 'Julian Barnes in Conversation' 262). Because great
works of literature live perpetually in the present when they are
activated in the minds of readers, for Geoffrey, Flaubert's writing has been a more reliable companion than Ellen, his sexually
unfaithful, psychologically unfathomable, and (in any event) now-
departed wife. Late in the novel, he characterizes her as 'someone I
feel I understand less well than a foreign writer dead for a hundred
years' (168). And yet, despite Flaubert's own resolve to efface himself from his fictions, despite his dictum, quoted in Barnes's novel,
that the 'artist must manage to make posterity believe that he never
existed' (86), Geoffrey discovers that the French novelist's books are
not enough, that he needs somehow to reconstitute Flaubert himself. The answer to the question that Geoffrey poses at the start of
the novel—'Why does the writing make us chase the writer?' (12)—
is that the writing alone does not compensate sufficiently for the
fact of mortality. Flaubert's novels have outlasted their creator, but,
even if they remain in print for many centuries to come, they will
not withstand the 'planet death' that Chris speaks of in *Metroland*
(55). And in any event, *Flaubert's Parrot* echoes the view expressed in
Barnes's first novel that art is separate from life. 'Books make sense
of life', says Geoffrey. 'The only problem is that the lives they make
sense of are other people's lives, never your own' (168). His efforts
as an amateur biographer are intended to counter the spectre of
death by going beyond the web of Flaubert's texts to resurrect, in

some fashion or other, the dead author himself. Although he is not religious, Geoffrey, in effect, wants to perform the miracle of bringing Gustave Flaubert back to life in language. In the end, however, Geoffrey is confronted with the paradox that, although biographies narrate the lives of people, in the end they are just more books made of words, not reincarnations of their subjects. Biographies, he discovers, are just as detached from life as any other form of literary art.

The would-be biographer Geoffrey's motivation in pursuing his elusive subject is similar to that of Bill Unwin, the protagonist and narrator of *Ever After*, which Graham Swift published in 1992.[4] Like Geoffrey, Bill is mourning the death by suicide of his wife, whom he suspects of having been sexually unfaithful to him. Lacking religious faith, Bill is, like Geoffrey, attracted to literature as a surrogate because of its power to withstand the ravages of time. Even humble, informal literary efforts, such as the private notebooks that Bill has inherited from his Victorian ancestor Matthew Pearce, are, in Bill's words, 'a small plea . . . for non-extinction. A life . . . beyond life' (221). Bill is similar to Geoffrey in attempting to find solace for the loss of his wife in his efforts as an amateur biographer. Bill's plan is to flesh out the notebooks with his own biographical narrative, 'to take the skeletal remains of a single life and attempt to breathe into them their former actuality' (100). The reanimated Matthew can then serve as a proxy for the deceased Ruth, just as Flaubert does for Geoffrey's Ellen. But both Barnes's Geoffrey and Swift's Bill discover that while books may contain traces of living people, they cannot replace living people. And, in any case, as both Geoffrey and Bill are chagrined to find, any biographical subject constructed in words is more an imaginative invention than a veridical representation. In Geoffrey's formulation, any ostensibly objective historical writing is actually 'autobiographical fiction pretending to be a parliamentary report' (90). It will probably say more about the psychological needs of the writer than it will, about the actuality of the past that it purports to reflect.

Flaubert's Parrot opens with a description of a statue of Flaubert that Geoffrey is observing during a visit to Rouen. Before Geoffrey plumbs the limits of language in attempting to reconstruct Flaubert discursively, he investigates the extent to which the material remnants of the past can connect us to the once-living reality of a long-dead writer. The lifeless effigy (not even the original statue, we are pointedly told) is austerely detached from its viewers, whose gaze it will not return (11). Although it is made of an alloy guaranteed not to rust, Geoffrey doubts its longevity: 'Nothing much else to do with Flaubert has ever lasted. He died little more than a hundred years ago, and all that remains of him is paper. Paper, ideas, phrases, metaphors, structured prose which turns into sound' (12). Nevertheless, Geoffrey cannot quell his desire for a more tangible link to the great writer.

'What makes us randy for relics?' he asks (12). His diction here, which implies that Flaubert is a kind of saint, is consistent with Donald Horne's contention that tourists are the modern equivalent of medieval pilgrims (9–10). The devotion of late-twentieth-century people such as Geoffrey to great writers as secular saints is a logical extension of their elevation of art to quasi-religious status. But Horne explains that the development of secular relics began in Italy as early as the fifteenth century, when the wealthy and powerful began to collect classical statues (14). The art museums that were built in the eighteenth and nineteenth centuries became secular temples (15), the destinations of tourist-pilgrims in search of enlightenment and transcendent experience. It is physiological evidence of this psychological transformation that Chris and Toni naively try to record in *Metroland*, when they observe visitors in London's National Gallery. The boys' expectation that something profound will happen in viewers' psyches is hardly surprising, since, in Horne's words, 'the art museums still maintain the holiness of paintings as authentic "relics", and their own sanctity as cathedrals' (16). The authority of art galleries and museums is derived from the authenticity of the items that they display. 'Authenticity,' says Horne,

> is the special magic of museums. . . . In a history museum, it is not that this is the *kind* of hat that Napoleon wore, but that this is the *very* hat Napoleon wore. Such an emphasis on authenticity provides a radiance of value and scarcity that hallows the object in itself, so that often a museum provides not an account of social processes but a collection of isolated objects, sacred in themselves. (16–17)

Horne's thoughts here are very suggestive in relation to Geoffrey's reactions to the artefacts associated with Flaubert that he sees in Rouen's Hôtel-Dieu. The part of the museum devoted to Flaubert contributes to what Horne refers to as modern tourism's 'cults of the dead—at the tombs, monuments and museums of secular saints' (17). There and at the pavilion that was once part of Flaubert's residence at Croisset, Geoffrey is able to inspect objects that conjure up for him the presence of the great writer. Such relics as the very glass from which the dying Flaubert took his last sip of water and the crumpled handkerchief with which he wiped his feverish forehead 'catch [Geoffrey's] heart' and make him feel that he 'has been present at the death of a friend' (21). The eponymous stuffed parrot that he sees at the Hôtel-Dieu—the model for Loulou, the parrot in Flaubert's *Un Coeur Simple* that the good-hearted, pious Félicité worships as the Holy Ghost—makes Geoffrey feel 'ardently in touch with this writer. . . . I was both moved and cheered' (16). The language that Barnes uses in an essay titled 'The Follies of Writer Worship' to describe his own reaction to seeing the same stuffed parrot during the trip that inspired him to write the novel is even more explicitly religious. He refers to the parrot as a 'relic' and, echoing Joyce, calls the sight of it 'a small epiphany' (3). In his transformed state, Geoffrey finds himself sharing a mental picture with Flaubert. Remembering the staring eyes of the bird later when he is back in his hotel, Geoffrey is irritated in the same way that Flaubert was during the time when the parrot sat on his writing desk (18). This sense of intimacy with Flaubert is a momentary bridging of the separation caused by death.

As readers of *Flaubert's Parrot* are aware, however, Geoffrey's illusion of having established a living connection to the dead writer is dispelled when, in the pavilion at Croisset, he sees the second stuffed parrot, also labelled as the very one borrowed by Flaubert during the composition of *Un Coeur Simple*. Barnes's description of his own parallel disillusionment, 'part Monty Python, part moral tale', is memorably pointed: 'The first parrot had made me feel in touch with the master. The second parrot mocked me with a satirical squawk. What makes you think you can seize hold of a writer that easily, it asked me, and pecked me sharply on the wrist for my presumption' ('Follies of Writer Worship' 3). The parrot's duplication has destroyed the claim to authenticity, discussed by Horne, on which the authority of museums rests. The implication, though, is that even authentic relics do not really contain magical properties that can connect us to the dead. As Alison Lee says, even the 'real' parrot would not give Geoffrey a genuine mystical insight into Flaubert (3). In the following passage, Geoffrey describes our disconnection from the living reality of the past metaphorically, on analogy with Frédéric Moreau's experience in Flaubert's *L'Education Sentimentale* of seeing a parrot's perch through a window while he wanders through the streets of war-ravaged Paris after the 1848 revolution:

> It isn't so different, the way we wander through the past. . . . All around is wreckage. These people never stopped fighting. Then we see a house; a writer's house, perhaps. . . . We look in at a window. Yes, it's true; despite the carnage some delicate things have survived. . . . A parrot's perch catches the eye. We look for the parrot. Where is the parrot? We still hear its voice; but all we can see is a bare wooden perch. The bird has flown. (60)

By this point in *Flaubert's Parrot*, the parrot has already been explicitly established as a symbol, 'an emblem of the writer's voice' (19). In light of this association, the significance of the above passage is clear. The writer's voice is no longer literally audible (unless its sound has been recorded electronically), but readers can reconstitute traces of that voice from the writer's extant texts. The writer, however, the living parrot who once incarnated that voice, has vanished. We cannot locate him through what Pateman calls 'metonymic identification' (*Julian Barnes* 28). This is what Geoffrey has tried unsuccessfully to do in communing with places and items that were once associated with Flaubert. In Dominick LaCapra's terms, borrowed from Freud, Geoffrey has been guilty of making a fetish of the parrot. LaCapra's thoughts in the following passage could easily be applied to Geoffrey's researches into Flaubert:

> [F]or Freud a fetish is a substitute for a lost object, and it is related to the quest for full identity and narcissistic unity. The archive as fetish is a literal substitute for the 'reality' of the past which is 'always already' lost for the historian. When it is fetishized, the archive is more than the repository of traces of the past which may be used in its inferential reconstruction. It is a stand-in for the past that brings the mystified experience of the thing itself—an experience that is always open to question when one deals with writing and other inscriptions. (92, n. 17)

As several critics have noticed, Geoffrey soon recognizes that one reason for his inability to establish a direct, living connection to Flaubert through material objects is that they need, inevitably, to be mediated through systems of signification, such as language, in order to have meaning. As James Scott says, rather than being 'signifying ends in themselves', artefacts are links in endless chains of meaning (60). The parrot borrowed by Flaubert, Geoffrey tells us, is not only caught up in the web of language; as a symbol of the writer's voice, it is also symbolic of language itself: 'You could say that the parrot, representing clever vocalisation without much brain power, was Pure Word. If you were a French academic, you might say that he was *un symbole du Logos.* . . . Is the writer much more than a sophisticated parrot?' (18) The parrot, then, far from being an unproblematic link to the reality of Flaubert, symbolizes a medium that is, according to Geoffrey, notoriously severed from whatever it purports to represent: 'We no longer believe that language and reality "match up" . . . congruently—indeed we probably think that words give birth to things as much as things give birth to words' (88). Inasmuch as language is polysemous, or, in Lee's words, 'inescapably plural' (39), the 'realities' that it conjures up are multiple, and sometimes contradictory, rather than singular. Peter Brooks gives the parrot's symbolism an overtly deconstructionist interpretation when he says that parrots

> speak only others' words, and (so far as we know) speak them without understanding, in an act of perfect imitation and inane transmission. The parrot is finally a highly troubling symbol for the logos, one that casts doubt on the assumed connection between intention and utterance. . . . It may be the writer's fate to make language express not himself but itself. This may be the final stage in artistic 'impersonality': the writer becomes the stage manager of language (3–4).

In bringing the problematics of linguistic representation explicitly to the fore, Barnes turns *Flaubert's Parrot* into a metafiction that is as much about its own status as a narrative made of words as it is about the inability of Geoffrey Braithwaite to come to terms with the loss of Ellen and his compensatory love for a great French novelist. Unlike Flaubert's unobtrusive narrators (who disappear by means of free indirect discourse into the characters of his novels), Geoffrey is flamboyantly intrusive, calling attention to his own presence in a fashion that disrupts the text's illusion of reality. Rather than enhancing the novel's verisimilitude, as Flaubert's invisible narrators do by creating the illusion that nothing stands between the readers and the characters, the situations and the events depicted, Geoffrey discourses openly on nineteenth- and twentieth-century narrative techniques, thereby exposing the artifices underlying fictional realism (89). Styling himself as 'a hesitating narrator' (89), he frequently interrupts his storytelling in order to comment self-consciously on the methods used to fabricate the text. The fragmentary, multi-generic character of the text that he presides over has the effect of reminding readers that there is no natural, single, totalizing means of representing the lives of individuals. Such demystifying tactics undermine the realism of *Flaubert's Parrot* without destroying it completely, a paradoxical state of affairs that Linda Hutcheon sees to be typical of metafiction; it is, she says, 'less a departure from the mimetic novelistic tradition than a reworking of it' (*Narcissistic* 5). This intention both to install and to trouble realism is displayed in Geoffrey's combination throughout the novel of an empirical attention to small, often trivial, details relating to Flaubert's biography and an extreme epistemological scepticism.

This paradoxical aspect of self-conscious fiction is also shown in the appearance within *Flaubert's Parrot* of both entirely fictional and 'real' characters, those based on historical personages, such as the nineteenth-century French writers Flaubert and Louise Colet and the twentieth-century academics Enid Starkie and Christopher Ricks. As Lee says, the effect of this mixing is to violate the boundary between what is usually thought to be discrete ontological levels. Made-up characters are treated as though they were real, and, conversely, real people are rendered fictional (46). In moments of frame-breaking, characters move from one level of reality to another. Pateman cites the example (on page 78 of the novel) of Geoffrey (a fictional character) criticizing his creator, Julian Barnes (a real person), for an error that he made about *Madame Bovary* in *Metroland* (*Julian Barnes* 25). And, of course, as Mélanie Joseph-Vilain reminds us (183), *Flaubert's Parrot* initially creates uncertainty about Geoffrey's status. Although we quickly infer that he is an invented character, in the prefatory note preceding the table of contents, Barnes affirms his narrator's actuality when he says that 'the translations in this book are by Geoffrey Braithwaite'.

The metafictional aspects of the novel are usually viewed as serving a pessimistic vision of life in which death is inevitable and final; truth is indistinguishable from fabrications; the past is available only in the form of multiple, contradictory narratives produced by people with faulty memories from limited, distorting perspectives; and human beings, fundamentally isolated, lack a real understanding of both themselves and those with whom they are most intimately connected. And yet it is possible to interpret the self-reflexive features of *Flaubert's Parrot* more affirmatively if we reflect on the ways in which they serve a dialogic attempt to make life as meaningful as possible in spite of its punishing limitations. One such metafictional tactic is to turn the reader into a character in the novel, who crosses the English Channel with Geoffrey in one chapter and in another accompanies Louise Colet on a walk while she tells her story. Both Gasiorek and Joseph-Vilain assert that this self-conscious highlighting of the reader's role is more cynically manipulative than truly dialogic, since Barnes does not record the views of this conspicuously silent listener (Gasiorek 161; Joseph-Vilain 186). But Joseph-Vilain does allow that, in transporting the reader metaleptically to what narratologists call the extradiegetic level of the narrative (the level at which the story is told), Barnes stresses his or her role as 'co-creator of the text' (186). Even as he makes the dramatized reader a hapless victim of the monologic rhetoric of Geoffrey and Louise, then, Barnes reminds his actual readers of their agency in activating narratives imaginatively and, when it is appropriate, in resisting their coercions.

In an obvious sense, the entire novel is a dialogue that Julian Barnes is conducting with Gustave Flaubert, inasmuch as the novel embeds his writing within Barnes's own. *Flaubert's Parrot* is thoroughly intertextual in containing many quotations from, allusions to, and parallels with Flaubert's literary works. Barnes himself, for example, has commented in an interview with Patrick McGrath on how he wanted Geoffrey's relationship with Ellen to echo that of Charles and Emma Bovary (23). There are allusions to and intertextual connections with the texts of other writers as well. Childs argues that Barnes has modelled Geoffrey on John Dowell, the narrator of Ford Madox Ford's modernist classic, *The Good*

Soldier (89), and Terence Rafferty claims that Barnes's novel is similar to Nabokov's *Pale Fire* in exhibiting the conventions of the 'criticism novel' (22). *Flaubert's Parrot* contains many 'voices', including those of historical figures such as Louise Colet, whom Barnes ventriloquizes in chapter 11, and invented characters such as Geoffrey and Ed Winterton, the deranged American academic who claims to have destroyed the letters which Flaubert and the English woman Juliet Herbert wrote to each other.

What is positive about the highly self-conscious dialogism of *Flaubert's Parrot* is that it represents not a defeatism in the face of the past's impenetrability but an honest recognition that it can only be known partially, from limited, ever-changing perspectives. The past may be, in Geoffrey's striking metaphor, 'a distant, receding coastline' that we view with varying degrees of accuracy from the deck of a constantly moving ship (101), but this does not mean that it cannot be seen at all. And, since no observer has a privileged, absolute vantage point, completeness can only be approached (however distantly) when many different versions of the past are assessed against each other and provisionally assembled in a variety of different discursive forms. According to LaCapra, all historiography is dialogical because 'the historian enters into a "conversational" exchange with the past and with other inquirers seeking an understanding of it' (36). Geoffrey's efforts to understand Flaubert are exemplary in LaCapra's terms because Geoffrey doesn't try to hide or suppress their dialogical character, as, according to LaCapra, traditional historians do. Furthermore, Barnes's writing is internally dialogized in the way that LaCapra recommends:

> the 'voice' of the historian may be internally 'dialogised' when it undergoes the appeal of different interpretations, employs self-critical reflection about its own protocols of inquiry, and makes use of modes such as irony, parody, self-parody, and humor, that is, double- or multiple-voiced uses of language. (36)

Geoffrey's pursuit of Flaubert represents 'the will to truth', not the 'will to fabulate' (Gasiorek 164) that Barnes discusses in the passage from *A History of the World in 10¹/₂ Chapters* quoted near the beginning of this chapter, although Geoffrey's biographical efforts *are* therapeutic in helping him deal with his unresolved feelings about Ellen. Conducting a dialogue with the dead is, as LaCapra admits, a strange activity (36); but Geoffrey finds it meaningful, even if it cannot bring them back to life. Pateman draws usefully on LaCapra's psychoanalytic model in explaining that Geoffrey benefits from a transferential 'process of self-identification from within which he can create a stable interpretive context for himself' ('Is There a Novel in this Text?' 44). In short, he is making sense of his own life in attempting to understand the elusive Flaubert and the enigmatic Ellen. In this regard, as several critics have pointed out, it is really a mark of Geoffrey's success, not his failure, that the task of constructing Flaubert's biography is endless, since it is the process that he has set in motion that is significant to him, not some finished product (Boccardi 156; Scott 62). He can never have direct, unmediated access to the past, but it is important to recognize that mediation is what prevents a schism from occurring, what allows him to make any link at all between his present and the past. Seen in this way, the postmodern self-consciousness of *Flaubert's Parrot* does not so much negate its own historical representations as it reveals what makes it possible to create them.

A HISTORY OF THE WORLD IN 10¹/₂ CHAPTERS

Like *Flaubert's Parrot*, *A History of the World in 10¹/₂ Chapters* sets out explicitly to demolish any confidence that readers might have in the objective, seamless truth of recorded history. *A History* flaunts a structural feature shared by many postmodernist works of fiction: textual fragmentation or deformation of a sort that is incompatible with a totalizing representation of the past. Both Claudia Kotte and Jackie Buxton have discerned that the book's half chapter undermines the experience of completeness (conventionally associated with the number ten) that would be part of the appeal of a truly universal history (Buxton 56). *Flaubert's Parrot* is like *A History* in being generically hybrid, but, as Gasiorek notes, Geoffrey's 'controlling consciousness' supplies the former novel with more unity than is displayed by *A History*, which has many narrators, not just one (159). This work more closely resembles a collection of diverse (albeit thematically related) short fictions than the novel that the book's dust jacket promises. Written from many different perspectives in a variety of stylistic registers and cast in incommensurable modes of writing, Barnes's text crosses ontological boundaries while refusing to construct a stabilizing hierarchy of meanings. As Kotte states, the novel's mixture of the factual and the fabulous violates the standard expectation that historiography must treat actual rather than fictional events ('Random Patterns' 108). Barnes's point in blending the mythical with the historical is the same one that Hayden White makes when he argues that 'we can only know the *actual* by contrasting it with or likening it to the *imaginable*' (*Tropics* 98). If this is so, if, as R. G. Collingwood asserted many years ago, the historian's understanding of the past is 'in every detail an imaginary picture' (245), then how could the actual ever finally be disentangled from the imaginable? As Barnes's narrator says in 'Three Simple Stories', in relation to a late nineteenth-century report of an incident remarkably similar to the story of Jonah being swallowed by the whale, '[m]yth will become reality, however sceptical we might be' (181).

Although many different kinds of discourses comprise *A History*, no single one achieves authority: not the convincing pastiche of an actual historical account from the early nineteenth century of the wreck of the French ship *Medusa*; not the transcript of a legal proceeding; nor even scripture, which is parodied in the form of a revisionist's retelling, from the point of view of a stowaway termite, of the story in Genesis of Noah and the Ark. No special status is achieved by the section of Barnes's book that seems to be written most directly from his own point of view as author: the disquisition on love in the half chapter, 'Parenthesis', in which he 'fret[s] at the obliquities of fiction' and seems to invite us to accept his thoughts as a heartfelt personal creed (225). Donald Pease is informative in observing that 'the term "author" raises questions about authority and whether the individual is the source or effect of that authority. The word "author" derives from the medieval term *auctor*, which denoted a writer whose words commanded respect and belief' (106). Pease goes on to explain that the individual genius of the modern author came to replace the cultural tradition of the medieval *auctor* as the sanction for the views of a literary work (108–11). Readers might be tempted to grant special authority to Barnes's views on love on the basis of his creativity and literary celebrity. Personal sincerity and deep feeling seem to ground his eloquent defence of love, but the very fact that his are avowedly personal views raises the spectre of their subjectivity. 'That's my theory, anyway' (241), says the narrator, defensively (with reference to the sexual indiscretions of politicians), thereby reminding us of the existence of competing, equally plausible theories.

Some of Barnes's discourses strive to be authoritative in other ways, but each is undercut by virtue of the overall context in which he places them: a postmodern one in which foundational or master narratives do not exist. Take, for example, the historical account in 'Shipwreck' of the ordeal suffered by the French seamen and passengers cast adrift on a raft after the frigate *Medusa* struck a reef in July 1816. Barnes tells us in the 'Author's Note' that for this part of 'Shipwreck' he drew 'its facts and language from the 1818 London translation of Savigny and Corréard's *Narrative of a Voyage to Senegal*' (308). Resting on the first-hand knowledge of the authors, who survived the disaster, this nineteenth-century source text seems to have considerable authenticity. The rhetoric that Barnes employs here is confident, emotionally poised, and even magisterial. As the following passage attests, the perspective is seemingly one that the authors, as participants, could not have had: that of a god who can look down on the raft and describe it with perfect equanimity, objectivity, and precision.

> The raft, which now carried less than one half of its original complement, had risen up in the water, an unforeseen benefit of the night's mutinies. Yet those on board remained in water to the knees, and could only repose standing up, pressed against one another in a solid mass. On the fourth morning they perceived that a dozen of their fellows had died in the night; their bodies were given to the sea, except for one that was reserved against their hunger. At four o' clock that afternoon a shoal of flying fish passed over the raft, and many became ensnared in the extremities of the machine. That night they dressed the fish, but their hunger was so great and each portion so exiguous, that many of them added human flesh to the fish, and the flesh being dressed was found to be less repugnant. Even the officers began to eat it when presented in this form. (120)

This is the sort of historical writing that, according to White, does not so much narrate as it 'narrativize[s]'. He coins this term in the process of distinguishing 'between a [narrated] discourse that openly adopts a perspective that looks out on the world and reports it and a [narrativized] discourse that feigns to make the world speak itself and speak itself *as a story*' ('Value of Narrativity' 6–7). In other words, writing of the kind quoted above serenely implies that it constitutes the complete objective truth, not a situated, fallible representation of the affair.

What undermines the authority of the historical narrative in the first part of 'Shipwreck' is nothing intrinsic to it but rather the second part, which deals, in a markedly more self-conscious style, with Theodore Géricault's famous painting of the raft (a colour photograph of it separates the two parts of 'Shipwreck'). In sensitizing us to the political context of the *Medusa* disaster (the conflict between Bonapartists and monarchists), the second part makes us realize that the narrative in the first part is misleadingly incomplete. The sense of authority that it communicates is an illusion created by rhetoric rather than a result of authentically godlike knowledge. Much has been excluded from both the narrative and the painting. Indeed, as Barnes's narrator points out, Géricault actually changed some of the factual details reported by Savigny and Corréard. '[W]hat is true is not necessarily convincing', the narrator explains (129). Even if it were as accurate as possible, no single representation could depict all of the details or encompass all of the possibly relevant considerations. Could any version, be it painted or written, satisfy the changing expectations and values that successive generations of viewers and readers might impose on such a narrative? Clearly, Barnes does not think so:

> Nowadays, as we examine [Géricault's] 'Scene of a Shipwreck,' it is hard to feel much indignation against Hughes Duroy de Chaumareys, captain of the expedition, or against the minister who appointed him captain, or the naval officer who refused to skipper the craft, or the soldiery who mutinied. (Indeed, history democratizes our sympathies. Had not the soldiers been brutalized by their wartime experiences? Was not the captain a victim of his own pampered upbringing? Would we bet on ourselves to behave heroically in similar circumstances?) (133)

Another type of writing that Barnes incorporates into the book is the legal transcript, which would seem by its very nature to command authority. The law has behind it the official imprimatur and power of the state. But such authority is not timeless, as Barnes reminds us by fabricating the transcript of an early sixteenth-century proceeding (based, he claims in the 'Author's Note', on a real case [308]) in France against woodworms that had infested a church and caused a bishop to be seriously injured when the damaged chair in which he sat collapsed. Although Barnes defends the medieval practice of trying non-humans for breaking human laws on the grounds that it was 'a sign of how wonderfully larger and more extended the sense of life was in those days' (Freiburg 56), by modern standards such trials are self-evidently absurd, since animals cannot possibly comprehend our laws. The advocate defending the woodworms does, in fact, make this point (65–66), but, because of the official position of the church in such a theocracy, in order to have a chance to plead his case successfully he needs to square his argument with Christian theology. So, in turn, does the prosecutor. All parties (the woodworms excepted, of course) accept scripture as a master narrative, something which the implied reader constructed by Barnes cannot do, for the satirical first chapter of A History totally discredits the account in Genesis of Noah's voyage, on which the arguments of both lawyers rest. And, in any event, 'The Wars of Religion' reminds us that even in sixteenth-century France the Bible did not speak its own meanings. They were then and are now the product of interpretations, and the bloody battles between Catholics and Huguenots (to which the title of Barnes's story refers) showed how violently irreconcilable competing interpretations may be.

As I said with reference to the self-reflexivity of Flaubert's Parrot, the textual heterogeneity and dismantling of master narratives in A History have two contradictory sets of implications, depending on whether we apply a deconstructionist logic or a Bakhtinian one. It would be possible to emphasize the inevitably fabricated nature of all historical representations—in other words, the baselessness of a world in which there is nothing outside the text—or, more hopefully, the opportunities for personal and political change given by a situation in which the meanings of language, however unstable, however unconnected to a 'transcendental signified', are generated by the actions of individuals and groups in society. Despite having some similarities to poststructuralism in their emphasis on what Patricia Waugh describes as the 'relational, open-ended and perspectival' nature of knowledge (59), Bakhtin's theories give more credence to human agency. The social and literary processes of dialogism (or polyphony) and the carnivalesque that his works expound are, effectively, strategies whereby ordinary people can resist, or at least protest, the coercions of the powerful. As David Lodge says, there 'is an indissoluble link between the linguistic variety of prose fiction, which [Bakhtin] called heteroglossia, and its cultural function as the continuous critique of all repressive, authoritarian, one-eyed ideologies' ('The Novel Now' 136).

The clash of voices and points of view in A History serves what Bakhtin perceived to be the pluralistic and democratic tendencies of the novel as a genre (Clark and Holquist 242–3). As I have mentioned, the author's voice is present in the text (in 'Parenthesis'), but it does not dominate monologically. On the contrary, his demystifying comments about recorded history undercut his own authority by constituting the sort of 'self-critical reflection' that LaCapra refers to as internally dialogized writing (36). Furthermore, Barnes allots less space for himself than he does for his characters. Some of them narrate their own stories, such as the desperate female protagonist of 'The Survivor' and the woodworm who has stowed away on Noah's Ark in the first chapter. No authorial mediation is detectable in these stories, or in 'Upstream!', which consists entirely of personal letters written in colourful, demotic prose by an actor making a movie in South America to his girlfriend in England. In these chapters, Barnes makes considerable use of irony, parody, and other forms of doubly-oriented discourse. 'Upstream!', for example, falls into the category of comic fiction mentioned by Bakhtin that features 'parodic stylisations of generic, professional and other languages' (Dialogic Imagination 302). The actor's extravagant, egocentric letters reveal fashionably bohemian attitudes, a roistering lifestyle, and views on acting that parody a recognizable stereotype: the actor as larger-than-life, passionate, existential hero.

What the dialogic collision of points of view permits in Barnes's A History is a contesting or even rewriting of standard or orthodox accounts of, or ways of thinking about, the past. In 'Stowaway', for instance, the insubordinate, irreverent voice of the woodworm counteracts the dogmatic, patriarchal voices of Noah and the Old Testament God. Like Kath, the narrator of 'Survivor', the woodworm is a passionate advocate of animal rights. It attacks the Judeo-Christian view that humans are superior to other animals by virtue of their special relationship to God, and it presents a version of life on the Ark that exposes Noah as a debauched monster who treated animals cruelly and exterminated entire species of them, not as the wise saviour, familiar from biblical tradition, of every form of life on earth. As Brian Finney notices (5), the prescient reindeer onboard the Ark, who worry about an unspecified future disaster, look ahead prophetically to the environmental concerns of Kath Ferris in 'The Survivor', who reports with horror that radioactive reindeer (victims of the Chernobyl nuclear accident) have been fed to mink. She explicitly supports the woodworm's charge against humanity: 'we've been punishing animals from the beginning, haven't we?' (87). Like the woodworm, Kath overturns orthodox ways of representing the past. She emphatically rejects the familiar 'Great Men' model of historiography: 'There was a battle here, a war there, a king was deposed, famous men—always famous men, I'm sick of famous men—made events happen. . . . I look at the history of the world . . . and I don't see what they see' (97). Christina Kotte elaborates on the revisionism of 'The Survivor' in pointing out that its two competing, equally plausible, explanations of what befell Kath subvert 'the notion of history as a "God-eyed version"', or a 'monological, harmonious whole' (87). Kotte also observes that Kath's substitution of what she sees as a female, cyclical, temporal reality for a linear one amounts to a dismissal of 'a teleological order of history, which is seen as a masculine force directed towards the future' (88).

In writing on the tendency of *A History* to present alternative versions of past events from the perspectives of history's marginalized and victimized, who thereby expose the injustice and tyranny that orthodox accounts elide, both Buxton and Gasiorek invoke Walter Benjamin's 'Theses on the Philosophy of History' rather than Mikhail Bakhtin's work (Buxton 57; Gasiorek 164). Like Benjamin's fragmentary, gnomic essay, Barnes's novel depicts the forces of history as violent and apocalyptic. Whereas Benjamin imagines history as one long catastrophe that 'keeps piling wreckage upon wreckage' (249), Barnes employs the recurrent metaphor of human history, from its very beginnings to the present, as a desperate voyage by boat or ship on which people are (usually vainly) seeking deliverance from various kinds of disasters. These vessels range from the aforementioned biblical Ark and raft of the

Medusa to twentieth-century ocean liners such as the *Titanic* and *St. Louis*, which in 1939 carried a cargo of Jewish refugees from Nazi Germany to ports in many countries that refused to accept them. Buxton claims that Barnes shares Benjamin's utopian hope for an ultimate redemption from the horror of history (61), but her contention does not square with her own subsequent recognition that *A History's* last chapter is 'a parodic dream of the messianic advent [hoped for by Benjamin], a satiric evocation of a paradise of conspicuous consumption that is, quite literally, bourgeois heaven' (80–1). It is true that in 'Parenthesis' Barnes does affirm the power of love to 'teach us to stand up to history', but it is important to acknowledge his emphatic denial that love can finally change its course (238). A few of the usually silenced losers in history's ruthless struggle are heard in Barnes's novel, but their revisionist narratives do not ameliorate its destructiveness.

Claudia Kotte argues persuasively that not only does Barnes undermine eschatological models of history, such as Benjamin's, which order 'history in consideration of its end' (113), but he also repudiates other familiar paradigms, such as Marx's materialist dialectic of progress and mythic, cyclical patterns, according to which the same primal events are repeated eternally. The many cruel ironies that circulate throughout *A History* discredit any belief in historical progress, such as that of Colonel Fergusson of 'The Mountain', or any hope that an investigation into history's origins and ends can disclose a redemptive principle. For characters in two of Barnes's fictions the quest for evidence of a providential design takes the form of a physical trek to Turkey's Mount Ararat, the fabled resting place of Noah's Ark. The nineteenth-century figure Amanda Fergusson in 'The Mountain' and the twentieth-century astronaut Spike Tiggler in 'Project Ararat' both hope to discover the Ark and, in doing so, receive a divine illumination with which to counter the secular, materialist times in which they live. But in casting doubt on the veracity of the biblical story of Noah and the Flood, the novel's first chapter has already conditioned readers to treat Amanda's and Spike's religious beliefs with scepticism. We are not surprised, therefore, when carbon dating proves that the bones found by Spike are those of a woman who died a century earlier, not those of Noah, as he believes. Readers are being invited to infer that what Spike has found are Amanda's remains. In that earlier story, after injuring herself (seemingly deliberately), she remains alone in a cave on Ararat in the sure belief that this suicidal decision is the will of God, who is poised to save her. We do not doubt the genuineness of her faith, but Barnes has placed us at an ironic remove from both Amanda and her modern counterpart, Spike. What Barnes does affirm is not the existence of God but rather the importance of religious beliefs in the chaotic and violent movements of history: 'God comes into [A] History of the World a lot because there has been a lot of God in the history of the world' (Freiburg 56).

Claudia Kotte argues that the novel also undermines the cyclical paradigm of history that both 'The Survivor' and 'Upstream!' could be read to affirm. In the first place, the authority of the narrators of both stories is clearly subverted. Kath may be mentally deranged to the point that she is hallucinating and hearing voices, and 'Upstream!' undercuts the naïve primitivism of its narrator, Charlie, who lionizes the simple authenticity of the South American Indians with whom he is working on a movie that closely resembles The Mission (1986). Like Kath, who believes that the 'old ways of doing things had to be rediscovered: the future lay in the past' (96), Charlie thinks that he is learning how best to live by observing the naturalness of the 'noble savages' who pilot the raft used in the historical film in which he is acting. Mounting evidence that they are not ideal gradually disillusions him, and his admiration for them ends abruptly when they, apparently intentionally, capsize the raft being used in the film causing the death of his co-star, Matt Smeaton. But Charlie's interpretation that the Indians believed that they were participating in a ritual re-enactment of an archetypal event could nevertheless lend support to the idea that in the novel Barnes is endorsing a cyclical model of historical processes: the eternal recurrence of the deluge and its catastrophic effects. Kotte shows, however, that Barnes stresses the singularity of each disaster in a way that counteracts a model of historical circularity ('Random Patterns' 122). She sums up by saying that

> the author highlights ruptures, subtle contradictions and inconsistencies, differences and conflicts. He thus vehemently rejects the metaphysical concept of history as the meaning of a pattern which unfolds and fulfils itself.... Instead, chance, coincidences and farcical as well as tragic ironies triumph over necessity and rationality. ('Random Patterns' 123)

A *History* implies that whatever patterns are discernible in the long sweep of historical events are the creations of those who represent them, not inherent properties of the events themselves. As I said earlier in the chapter, the novel sensitizes readers to the fabrications, distortions, and omissions that taint all historical writing and representations in other media, such as Géricault's painting. Barnes's demystifying metafictional devices cast doubt upon the veracity of all such images and emplotments, but nevertheless Barnes sees value in them, especially in those which are aesthetically accomplished. They provide at least the illusion that we can understand and even master the murderous onslaught of history. Out of something horrible comes something wonderful. 'Why did it happen', Barnes's narrator asks in 'Parenthesis', 'this mad act of nature, this crazed human moment? Well, at least it produced art. Perhaps, in the end, that's what catastrophe is *for*' (125). What Géricault captured on canvas 'is no reducing process. It is freeing, enlarging, explaining' (137). But, as Gregory Rubinson perceives (102), Barnes sees the painting's triumph as contingent, not transcendent. As he did in *Metroland* and *Flaubert's Parrot*, he feels compelled to deflate the traditional ideal of art's immortality, however much he might like to subscribe to it:

> And there we have it—the moment of supreme agony on the raft, taken up, transformed, justified by art, turned into a sprung and weighted image, then varnished, framed, glazed, hung in a famous gallery to illuminate our human condition, fixed, final, always there. Is that what we have? Well, no. People die; rafts rot; and works of art are not exempt.... Our leading expert on Géricault confirms that the painting is 'now in part a ruin'.(139)

History, then, whether in the form of sudden catastrophe or slow decay, finally overtakes all attempts to stop or rise above its flux. The representation of history becomes a part of history, not a refuge from its ravages. Another example of this phenomenon is depicted in 'Upstream!'. As I mentioned, one of the two leading actors is killed during the filming of a movie closely based on historical accounts of a journey by raft up a South American river undertaken by two Jesuit priests. The scene sabotaged by the Indians was supposed to depict one priest saving the other after the raft overturned. With Matt's drowning, this attempt to 'turn catastrophe into [cinematic] art' (125) becomes merely another of history's fatal catastrophes, just as the endeavour to understand and communicate the patterns and meanings of history is engulfed by its violence in 'The Visitors', when Franklin Hughes, who is employed to give historical lectures on a cruise ship, is forced at gunpoint by Arab terrorists to give the passengers a historical justification of their plan to execute two of them every hour until the terrorists' demands have been met. Hughes does as he is told, and numerous members of his audience are subsequently slaughtered before the terrorists are overcome by the American Special Forces.

History's brutality cannot, in Barnes's view, be transcended by means of religious practices or transformed by means of the intellect or creative imagination. As Pateman says, Barnes shows that religion is 'too much a part of the world', too co-opted by its history, 'to be any good to people wanting relief' (*Julian Barnes* 47). And, as we have seen, art is equally flawed, for all of its appeal. Even that appeal is not universal, as Barnes admits in 'Parenthesis', for art 'isn't accessible to all, [and] where accessible isn't always inspiring or welcome' (243). His conclusion is that 'religion and art must yield to love', which humanizes us and instils in us a devotion to truth (243). Love, however, is not absolute; amorphous, elusive, and fallible, it will inevitably fail. When it does, says Barnes, 'we should blame the history of the world' (244).

ENGLAND, ENGLAND

England, England is a satiric fantasy designed to show how England is losing the knowledge of its own history by following what Fredric Jameson calls the postmodernist cultural logic of late capitalism. Unlike Jameson, however, who seems to believe as a Marxist that real historical knowledge can be acquired, Barnes in his novel offers no strong alternative to what Jameson characterizes as the 'blank parody' constituted by postmodernist representations of history: depthless, stereotypical images drawn, without a context of analysis, from past eras and mixed promiscuously (17–18). As both Randall Stevenson and Dominic Head point out, the novel does contain energies opposed to the blatant fabrications of English history and folklore sold to tourists in Sir Jack Pitman's theme park (Head 120; Stevenson 48), but what Stevenson calls Barnes's 'historical sympathies . . . for supposedly straightforward, bygone decencies of life in the English countryside' (48) are vexed by the same impediments to an objective understanding of the past that I discussed in the sections of this chapter on *Flaubert's Parrot* and *A History of the World in 10¹/₂ Chapters*. In particular, Barnes stresses the unreliability of memory as a tool for reconstructing the past. As he does in those earlier novels, he disputes the idea that we can gain unmediated access to the reality of earlier epochs, and he undermines the notion that nations can discover points of origin that explain and justify their own development through time. As Dr Max, the theme park's official historian, asserts,

> there *is* no authentic moment of beginning, of purity. . . . We may choose to freeze a moment and say that it all 'began' then, but as an historian I have to tell you that such labelling is intellectually indefensible. What we are looking at is almost always a replica. . . . There is no prime moment. (135)

Implicated in it though he may be, Dr Max is utterly contemptuous of the England, England project that the novel satirizes, and consequently his views on history have a certain authority. They do not seem distanced by irony from those of Barnes himself.

The novel draws a parallel between the ways in which nations and individuals fashion their own histories. Dr Max makes this equation explicitly when he tells the protagonist, Martha Cochrane, that national and personal identities are alike in being constructed or even stolen rather than being uncovered or discovered (136–7). Barnes speaks of this theme in an interview (and in the process alludes to the title of an influential book edited by Eric Hobsbawm and Terence Ranger) when he tells Penelope Dening that 'I am interested in what you might call the invention of tradition. Getting its history wrong is part of becoming a nation. And we do the same thing with our lives. We invent, ransack and reorder our childhood' (2). One reviewer even suggests that Martha personifies England in this regard (Wiegand 3).

But Martha's biography is certainly not intended to be anything like an allegory of the historical trajectory that Barnes charts for England over the course of the novel. In the same interview quoted above, he makes it clear that her private story is, in part, intended as a contrast to what unfolds on the public, national level:

> There are these disparities and opposing extremes running through the book between the public and the private, between the fake and the authentic.... And what's happening in the public story is the creation of something that is completely false and what's going on in the private story is the search for some sort of inner truth about life and love. (1–2)

The problem for Martha, however, is that in her quest for personal meaning she encounters the same epistemological barriers that Sir Jack and others use as pretexts to justify the gross falsity of England as it is replicated on the Isle of Wight. She is unable to find an unequivocal *raison d'être*, but her private struggle is worthy of respect in being an anguished search for reality—not a cynical abandonment of it for profit, of the sort in which she participates on the public level.

Barnes's novel shows how formulations of Englishness are especially prominent in the lucrative tourism industry, for, as Stevenson notes, 'a nation's sense of identity is inevitably entangled with images it has to adopt in presenting itself to the outside world' (47). Stevenson goes on to identify a contradictory facet of this conjunction, one that *England, England* exaggerates for satiric purposes, when he points out that 'pressures on English identity in the 1990s ... coincided awkwardly with a new need to turn English culture into foreign exchange, sometimes making artificial ... the very authenticities that "heritage" supposedly sought to sustain' (48). Barnes's novel, however, goes beyond illustrating Stevenson's point that there are financial incentives for the tourist industry to adulterate authenticity with artificiality. As I have already intimated, in *England, England* Barnes deconstructs the very concept of authenticity, showing how it is inextricably mixed with and dependent upon inauthenticity. Jonathan Culler offers a semiotic understanding of this paradox when he explains that a sense of authenticity derives from the framing of tourist sights by what Dean MacCannell in *The Tourist* labelled 'markers'. Culler defines them as 'any kind of information or representation that constitutes a sight as a sight: by ... making it recognizable' (159). Because they serve as markers, representations and replications are, according to Culler, what make a given tourist experience seem original or authentic (164). Consequently, the 'paradox, the dilemma, of authenticity, is that to be experienced as authentic it must be marked as authentic, but when it is marked as authentic it is mediated, a sign of itself, and hence lacks the authenticity of what is truly unspoiled, untouched by mediating cultural codes' (164). In the absence of replicas and other markers, in other words, an authentic experience would be unintelligible as an authentic experience.

According to Donald Horne, the quest of modern tourists for authentic contact with the historical past reflects a 'crisis in reality' (21), but, as Barbara Korte points out, 'in a time that is *post*modern, tourists may no longer even desire to find the authentic; *mock* authenticity, *surface* authenticity[,] seems to be satisfactory' (290). Barnes himself cites the example of the Venetian Hotel in Las Vegas, which was just being built when he was interviewed (Lanchester A5). In the Venetian, patrons can see the sights of central Venice without sacrificing the comfort of air conditioning, the excitement of gambling, and the ability to shop in the upscale stores that line the corridors. In a like fashion, Sir Jack's Isle of Wight project dispenses with authenticity altogether, becoming, in the fashionable jargon of Jean Baudrillard, hyperreality: a collection of simulacra that have replaced the reality of England and its history entirely. The process by which, in the words of Mark, Sir Jack's Project Manager, 'the real becomes the replica' (63) involves the structuralist logic discussed in the above paragraph. England, England manipulates the relationship between tourist sights and markers in a fashion that is discussed by MacCannell. Because of what he identifies as 'the *interchangeability* of the signifier and signified' in semiotic systems (118), markers can acquire the status of sights in their own right, and sights can become markers (117–23). Markers and sights are not different in kind from one another because '[t]he referent of a sign is another sign' (118). As Korte observes (286), the items generated by market research that comprise Sir Jack's list of Fifty Quintessences of Englishness—and serve as a blueprint for the theme park—are just such semiotic signs. Markers of England, such as warm beer, London taxis, and replicas of Big Ben, Stonehenge, and the Tower of London, become sights in their own right. Head believes that this phenomenon constitutes a 'false metonymy', whereby the 'symbols of England' are confused with the reality with which they are associated (124), but, as the disclosure of Anglia's fabricated national identity in its final section shows, Barnes's novel suggests that social 'reality' is inevitably constructed by means of invented symbols and metonymic linkages. Despite its reversion to a pre-industrial condition, Anglia is no organic community that has rediscovered its natural innocence. The first of its inhabitants to whom we are introduced is an immigrant from Milwaukee who masquerades as a crusty local countryman and makes up folktales to tell to visitors. Barnes offers no alternative to the manufacture of tradition.

England, England does differ from Anglia, though, in the calculating, crudely obvious character of its fabricated, 'living' history, which has been created and fine-tuned for the sole purpose of maximizing profit. The project is consistent with Culler's claim that 'modern tourism, with its reduction of cultures to signs . . . is a mask for the capitalist world system, a celebration of signification and differentiation which conceals the economic exploitation and homogenisation that underlies it' (167). The novel attacks the political and economic ideology that drives the Project and renders it grossly manipulative of its employees and customers (the Island, being a pure market state, has no citizens, and therefore no democracy or human rights). The wealthy vacationers from abroad, who spend their dollars and yen, and the workers who portray the figures drawn from English history and mythology are as interchangeable as the bumpers on Honda Accords. If Nell 1, the Island's designation for the actress portraying King Charles II's mistress Nell Gwynn, is unavailable, Nell 2 or Nell 3 can replace her. The Island treats people like fully decentred, postmodern subjects, and they frequently behave as though they do indeed lack any depth of personal identity. Korte instantiates the actors who identify with their roles so completely that they become the figures that they are impersonating (292). The actors playing Dr Johnson and Robin Hood and his band demonstrate the principle upon which England, England is based: they are simulacra that have displaced reality.

The caricatured depiction of English history on the Isle of Wight is calculated to agree with what patrons remember having learned about the nation's past. The Project's Official Historian has been hired not to ensure that the dramas enacted on the Island are faithful to the richness and complexity of British history, but, as the Concept Developer informs Dr Max, to ascertain what potential customers already 'know' about the subject: 'people won't be shelling out to *learn* things. . . . They'll come to us to enjoy what they already know' (74). Dr Max discovers that what they remember having learned consists only, in the words of Vera Nunning, of 'names, dates or meaningless catch-phrases' (66). As both Nünning and Korte have pointed out, Barnes stresses the fallibility of memory in providing for both individuals and nations continuity between the past and the present (Korte 292–3; Nünning 61). The sense of identity conferred by memory is, therefore, untrustworthy. Martha diagnoses the inherent weakness of memory at the novel's outset when she posits that it is always removed, in a *regressus in infinitum*, from the reality that it purports to contain:

> If a memory wasn't a thing but a memory of a memory of a memory, mirrors set in parallel, then what the brain told you now about what it claimed had happened then would be coloured by what happened in between. It was like a country remembering its history: the past was never just the past, it was what made the present able to live with itself. (6)

According to this line of thinking, historical understanding is always perspectival; it will always be contaminated by 'presentism', the false belief excoriated by Dr Max 'that the past is really just the present in fancy dress' (199). In this regard, what the Island offers is typical of heritage tourism, as Horne describes it: 'Anachronism . . . is the very essence of tourism: the present is used to explain the relics of the past, and then the meanings given to the past are used to justify aspects of the present' (29). It is sobering to think that even respectably scholarly approaches to history, of the sort that Dr Max would respect, are compromised, for '[h]istorians rely on the memories of others when it comes to sources. . . . The practice of history is, after all, a highly specialized form of commemoration. Yet we need to problematise the very notion of memory,' which is 'imperfect, producing "recollections" that simply cannot be true' (Jordanova 138).

The full reality of Martha's own past is as inaccessible to her as England's is to its residents and visitors. Just as England's history is rendered mythical in the theme park by the inclusion of idealized figures such as Robin Hood, so her earliest memories fictionalize her childhood, prior to her father's abandonment of the family, as a pastoral idyll. Despite her scepticism about these memories, she cannot stop herself from conjuring from the recesses of her mind a golden, Edenic day, during which 'nothing had gone wrong' (8), spent at a country fair with her parents. She is fascinated and comforted by the various horticultural competitions, particularly by the 'calm organization' and 'completeness' of the lists displayed that describe them (9). The exquisite regularity and vivid colours of Mr. Jones's prize-winning beans, which 'glowed in her mind . . . like holy relics', suggest the perfection of nature (10). Martha's memory combines for readers not only the idea of her innocence as a young child but also of England's rural bounty. Unspoiled, original identities are suggested for both Martha and the environment into which she is harmoniously integrated.

The scene at the agricultural show depicted in the novel's first part, however, contains dialogue between Martha's parents that gently mocks her assumptions and undercuts her idealization of the fair as a place 'with order, and rules, and wise judgement from men in white coats, like doctors' (18). She is expelled from her imagined Eden when her father leaves her and her mother, taking with him (Martha believes) one piece of her Counties of England jigsaw, thereby making it impossible for her to complete it. Several critics have noted that the lost piece representing Nottinghamshire associates her fall from grace and psychic wholeness with England's incomplete identity. Head remarks that Martha's 'loss of faith in the Counties of England jigsaw, with its bald certitude about the composition of England, signals a haziness about origins' (120), and Korte observes that 'the puzzle [is] an obvious image for the postmodern idea that all nations are constructs' (288–9). Since the novel makes a direct link between England's national identity and Martha's personal one, Barnes seems to be inviting readers to infer that individual identity is also a construction.

And indeed, Martha seeks purposely through the various stages of her life to fashion a self that is whole and fulfilled, to find meanings with which to fill her inner vacancy. She has no interest, in this connection, in art, one of the three potentially redemptive aspects of life discussed by Barnes in 'Parenthesis', but she does explore the other two: religion and love. Like many people, she has what could be broadly defined as a spiritual capacity, an ability to experience moments that seem sacred, but from early childhood on she is highly sceptical of the claims of organized religion. 'Martha was a clever girl', the narrator tells us, 'and therefore not a believer' (13). Her punishment in school for turning the Lord's Prayer into nonsense verse—being made to 'counterfeit an ardent faith' while leading the school in prayer—only makes her more cynical (14). Until she begins an affair with her fellow Pitco executive Paul Harrison, Martha is also disillusioned by her attempts to complete herself in sexual relationships with men. Readers are not surprised to learn how unsatisfactory these have been, for they already know that she has been primed by the trauma of her father's departure and by the subsequent teachings of her mother to find men either wicked or weak and to use her sex appeal to exact vengeance for wrongs done to her.

Of all her lovers, Paul alone seems, for a time, to offer a relationship approaching the ideal that she had formulated as a young woman. Her experience with him seems to validate her youthful 'assumption that completeness was possible, desirable, essential— and attainable only in the presence and with the assistance of Another' (51). Each finds in the other a genuineness that is nowhere apparent in their working life amidst the simulacra of England, England. 'I just think you're . . . real,', Paul tells her simply. 'And you make me feel real' (138). Martha's only hope of completing herself through love depends upon compartmentalizing her life rigidly. She tries to keep her private and public selves wholly separate, after the fashion of Wemmick in Dickens's *Great Expectations*. This proves impossible, and job-related pressures cause the couple's relationship to disintegrate. 'Why was everything back to front?' Martha wonders. 'She could make the Project work, even though she didn't believe in it; then, at the end of the day, she returned home with Paul to something she believed in, or wanted and tried to believe in, yet didn't seem able to make work at all' (197). The destruction of the relationship is complete when Paul participates in the conspiracy to depose her as Pitco's CEO and reinstate Sir Jack. She is finally forced to conclude that 'love was not the answer for her' (233).

Martha has failed, then, to create a solid identity through her love for Paul, and she is even driven to seek guidance from the anguished, mentally deranged 'Dr Johnson', who 'behaved as if she were less real than he was' (218). Her quest for authentic self-hood founders on the contradiction that, whereas she believes that 'happiness depended on being true . . . to your nature' (232), that 'nature' might well be indecipherable or even illusory: 'what if this nature were no more natural than the nature Sir Jack had satirically delineated after a walk in the country' (233)? If the self is a social construction, in other words, can it meaningfully be said to have a nature?

Barnes makes it plain near the end of the novel's long middle part, however, that Martha's search for meaning has not been entirely in vain. Two scenes that unfold in a deserted churchyard, clearly derived from Philip Larkin's 'Churchgoing', disclose that her suffering itself has a reality similar to that of the actor who believes that he is Dr Johnson: 'his pain was authentic because it came from authentic contact with the world' (223). In an environment of hyperreality, Martha's emotional pain at least is genuine, and this creates in her a need for salvation that is to some degree satisfied by communing with what the church once signified. Like the speaker of Larkin's poem, she is a non-believer who nevertheless finds in the church building evidence of 'a capacity for seriousness' that has been lacking in her life (243). 'Dr Max did not believe in salvation', Barnes's narrator tells us, 'but perhaps she did, and felt she might find it among the remnants of a greater, discarded system of salvation' (243). Again like Larkin's churchgoer, she communes with the dead who had been buried in the churchyard. They evoke in her a metaphysical interest in what, if anything, exists after death: 'What brought her here? She knew the negative answers: disappointment, age, a discontent with the thinness of life. . . . There was something else as well, though: a quiet curiosity bordering on envy. What did they know, these future companions of hers?' (226)

The novel leaves ambiguous the answer to the question of whether Martha moves any closer to deliverance in the last phase of her life in Anglia. Just as Barnes does not idealize Anglia as the rediscovery of England's aboriginal purity, so Martha, in solitary old age, has found no unequivocal self-definition or meaning in life. Too wise ever to be satisfied with the banal recipes for happiness that were on offer in the consumerist society that she chose to leave behind, Martha also recognizes the artificialities of the supposedly more traditional, natural way of life that Anglia has adopted. In response to the reproach of one of the villagers—'I thought you were one of us'—Martha replies, 'Perhaps I've known too many us-es in my time' (254). The Martha of the novel's final section is, indisputably, more serene, but this might be due to nothing more profound than the aging process: 'She no longer debated whether or not life was a triviality, and what the consequences might be if it were. Nor did she know whether the stillness she had attained was proof of maturity or weariness.' (266)

The village fête with which the novel concludes parallels the agricultural fair that Martha attends in Part 1 as a small child and lends to the novel's conclusion a celebratory quality counterbalancing the elegiac point of view from which it is experienced: that of an old woman nearing the end of her life. Although Barnes's narrator identifies the village itself as 'neither idyllic nor dystopic' (265), Head is right to say that the fête 'approaches a pastoral idyll. What is significant is how Barnes pushes the cliché—and in this sense the conclusion is a self-conscious fabrication like the rest of the book—until we begin to expect that it may deliver something of value after all' (121). What is valuable is not merely the serenity of Martha that Head goes on to mention but also the carnivalesque *joie de vivre* exhibited by the revellers. Readers cannot help but notice that the villagers masquerade as some of the same characters from English history and mythology impersonated in Sir Jack's theme park. What in England, England amounts to nothing more than a superficial, postmodernist culture of spectacle,[5] a flattening out of the past into mere visual display sold as a commodity, in Anglia takes the form of a populist carnival that has some of the liberating characteristics extolled by Bakhtin in *Rabelais and His World*. The masquerading exemplifies the playfulness, the openness to change, and the fluidity of identity that Bakhtin praises (39–40). It is true that, as a representation of English history, the carnival reveals the same indifference to and ignorance of the complex actuality of the past that is evident in England, England. Nevertheless, there is something positive in the double vision of the children, who express a

> willing yet complex trust in reality . . . so that even when they disbe-lieved, they also believed. . . . They saw all too easily that Queen Victoria

was no more than Ray Stout with a red face and a scarf round his head, yet they believed in both Queen Victoria and Ray Stout at the same time. (273–4)

The dualistic mindset of the children suggests an ability to accept the fabrications of individual and national identities as necessary fictions that need not wholly destroy our capacity to experience life as real. As Head states, this simultaneous habitation of both the present and an invented past

> might be said to sidestep the question of what an English national iden-tity should actually comprise; but it does indicate the spirit, complex and contradictory, in which such a project would need to be conducted, and which Barnes's novel, with mixed modes and counterpointed moods, nicely emulates' (121).

In satirizing the bogusness of England as it is presented for tourists on the Isle of Wight, Barnes employs a high degree of formal artifice in devising the plot, characters, themes, and other textual elements. As Ian Sansom observes, '*England, England* . . . is a book which not only poses questions about integrity and authen-ticity, but is itself something of a poser' (31). Sansom explains that the novel feels artificial because it draws heavily on topoi from the literary tradition, and he even claims that the central conceit of the novel, the reassembly of England in more compact form on a small island, has been 'poached' from a book written decades ago by Clough Williams-Ellis (31).[6] Pateman notices that Barnes's novel is also derivative of his own earlier works. He claims that this bor-rowing is so excessive that it damages *England, England,* which 'reads like the miniaturized, condensed, safe, easily accessible island world of Barnes's other books' (*Julian Barnes* 73). For Pateman, the prob-lem is that the novel succumbs to the fallacy of imitative form, and the result for the reader is a literary experience that is just as hollow as the object of the novel's attack: 'it might be possible to claim that Barnes . . . is himself deploying the strategies of simu-lacra, inauthenticity, and fake in order to tell a story of simulacra, inauthenticity, and fake' (75). In opposition to Pateman, however, I would argue that the rich intertextuality of *England, England* stands in contrast to the vapid imitativeness of Sir Jack's Island and could even be said to constitute a positive value against which the satire can be measured. Nünning observes correctly that Englishness, as it is constructed in the theme park, relies very little on the nation's literature, which is reproduced only in clichéd images of a select few authors and characters, such as Lawrence's Connie Chatterly (66). (The only three-dimensional representation, that of Dr Johnson, is popular with neither the Island's tourists nor its administrators.) Nünning is mistaken, though, in saying that intertextual references are lacking in the novel itself (66), which, as I have said, is far from the case. Virtually a work of *bricolage*, *England*, *England* has the emotional and intellectual depth to show that postmodernist narrative techniques do not always result in Jameson's 'blank parody'.

5

BEFORE SHE MET ME,
TALKING IT OVER,
AND LOVE, ETC.

LOVE, TRUTH, AND VIOLENCE

Matthew Pateman highlights the importance of love as a value for Barnes, claiming that it is for the novelist 'the potential basis of an ethics' ('Popularity of Ethics' 181). While Barnes has in fact identified himself as a moralist (McGrath 23), it is fair to say that most of his fictions treat romantic love as a source of confusion and anguish, not of ethical guidance. Pateman's argument rests heavily upon his reading of 'Parenthesis', but even that paean to love acknowledges that it will not make us happy (229). And, although the essayist of the famous half chapter claims that love is intimately connected to truth (238), it is usually the subjectivity and ephemerality of love as an experience that Barnes's fictions emphasize. In previous chapters of this study, I have focused on passages that breed doubt about the ontological status of romantic love, and the three books grouped together in this one also question its objective existence. If love is real and enduring, why, in *Talking It Over*, does Gillian stop loving Stuart? Or, to phrase the question more accurately, why does she come to love Oliver more than she does Stuart? For, in the sequel, *Love, etc.*, Gillian claims that her love for both men was genuine and strong: 'The point is, you can love two people, one after the other, one interrupting the other, like I did. You can love them in different ways. And it doesn't mean one love is true and the other is false' (16). Given the pain that Gillian inflicts on Stuart, we could conclude that their love proves to be more of an ethical quagmire than an ethical foundation. In Oliver's succinct formulation, '[e]very love story begins with a crime' (*Love, etc.* 14), and the gruesome finale of *Before She Met Me* could be cited as evidence that some end with one as well.

Love, for Barnes, is clearly not Shakespeare's transcendent, neo-Platonic 'ever-fixéd mark/That looks on tempests and is never shaken' (134). All of Barnes's works presuppose a general state of affairs of relativity. In his fictional world, humans do not have access to absolutes, including Love with a capital letter. In Shakespeare's Sonnet 116, 'Love's not Time's fool', despite the fact that the 'rosy lips and cheeks' of the lovers themselves must eventually fade and die (134). In 'Parenthesis', however, Barnes denies that love endures: 'When the survivor of a loving couple dies, love dies too. If anything survives of us, it will probably be something else' (226). Barnes affirms the reality of love, but he makes it quite clear that its ontological purchase is contingent and fragile. Is love, the narrator of 'Parenthesis' asks, '[s]omething pleasant, complex, but inessential? A random development, culturally reinforced, which just happens to be love rather than something else? I sometimes think so' (233).

Love, in Barnes's fictions, is problematic because the identities of the individuals whose behaviour is driven by the phenomenon are fraught in various ways. In contrast, when Shakespeare begins Sonnet 116 by saying 'Let me not to the marriage of true minds/Admit impediments' (134), he implies that the lovers, by virtue of their 'true minds', their God-given souls, have essential definition as people. Subject though they may be to the imperfections of the flesh, they can nonetheless be guided in life by a spiritual ideal of love. Barnes's characters, in contrast, lack this sort of foundation. How can the love that they experience be stable if their own identities are shadowy, multiple, and shifting? In *Talking It Over* Gillian asks, 'if two such different people as Stuart and Oliver can both fall in love with me, what sort of *me* is it? And what sort of *me* falls in love first with Stuart and then with Oliver? The same one, a different one' (176)?

In the case of *Before She Met Me*, the protagonist, Graham Hendrick, never wavers in his devotion to his wife, Ann, who is equally faithful to him, but his emotions assume such obsessive and perverse forms that they seem the result less of a 'true mind' than of a disordered brain controlled by its unevolved parts. In the novel, Barnes has stated, he played with a theory that the human brain contains within it two other brains, one lower mammalian and one reptile (McGrath 21). Its originator, the psychologist Paul D. MacLean, is quoted on the subject in one of the novel's epigraphs. It is ironic that the character who propounds the theory within the novel, Jack Lupton, becomes the victim of Graham's murderous, atavistic jealousy in a chapter titled 'The Horse and the Crocodile'. Pateman is right to say that Barnes's dramatization of MacLean's theory 'locates Hendrick within a strongly materialist conception of the self—a conception where the self is given (or at least heavily determined by) biological and neuro-physiological factors' (*Julian Barnes* 14).

In 'Parenthesis', as I stated in the previous chapter, Barnes's persona opposes the humanizing force of love to history's destructiveness, but the three novels discussed in this chapter actually suggest the contradictory idea that love is immersed in and subject to history, not separated from it. Ann Hendrick in *Before She Met Me*, for example, who had unthinkingly assumed that 'sex had always been like it is now' (104), learns from conversations with her historian-husband, Graham, that social practises to do with sex have altered radically with the centuries. All human relationships, including those between lovers, are social constructions that grow out of historically contingent narratives and paradigms. Since those relationships change with time, our knowledge of their past is limited by the same factors that undermine any other record of history. Charles Nicholl makes this point in comparing *Talking It Over* with two of its predecessors, *Flaubert's Parrot* and *A History of the World in 10½ Chapters*. What he says of *Talking ItOver* applies equally to *Before She Met Me* and *Love, etc.*:

> It asks the same nagging historical questions [as do *Flaubert's Parrot* and *A History of the World in 10½ Chapters*]. How do we know what really happened? How can anyone, even someone who was there, say what it was really like? In this case, the event itself, the bit of history that we are dealing with, is small [and] private. (19)

As he does in *England, England*, in these three novels of jealousy and betrayal, Barnes stresses the unreliability of memory and the subjectivity of any interpretation of past events.

BEFORE SHE MET ME

The second of Barnes's books published under his own name, *Before She Met Me* is a clever novel of ideas written within a hybrid genre combining comedy with melodrama and macabre violence. It is, as Gary Krist points out, as if Barnes has married the fictional worlds of Kingsley Amis and David Lodge on the one hand and the much darker one of James M. Kain on the other (1). This mixing of what might be thought to be radically incompatible modes is not uncommon in postmodernist fiction and films, and, as Moseley states, it bears particular comparison with work done by two of Barnes's contemporaries: Martin Amis and Ian McEwan (54). The justification that Amis offers for the mongrelized genre in which he works could easily be applied to Barnes's novel:

> The reason why comedy looks so odd is that tragedy doesn't exist anymore, it doesn't resonate—no one's going to believe in it anymore. So comedy is having to take on all the real ills, the refugees from other genres. The original butts of comedy used to be buffoonery, pretension, pedantry, but now they have to include murder and child abuse, the decay of society. Dickens, a comic writer of another age, dealt with his villains by either tritely punishing them or improbably converting them. But the old schema no longer work[s]. We know that evil isn't necessarily punished any more than good is rewarded. (53)

As Jack's mocking reference to Graham as 'the little Othello' implies (67), he more closely resembles a stock comic figure than a tragic hero. And yet, like Othello, possessed by jealousy, he commits a savage murder. Conventionally bourgeois, sexually timid and henpecked by his first wife, Graham is presented for much of the novel as the comic victim of instincts and emotions that he can neither understand nor control. When he finally does act on these feelings by repeatedly stabbing his friend Jack with a knife and then slitting his own throat, it seems less to the reader that an evil has been enacted and punished than that the bestial reality beneath the civilized surface of human life has been bathed in a lurid, darkly comic light. Barnes exposes this elemental brutality all the more effectively by making Graham an unthreatening, kind, eminently sensible individual, not a pugnacious hothead. The implication is that if even Graham descends to violence, its trigger might well be hard-wired genetically into our species.

As the grisly climax of the narrative suggests, then, the ideas that Barnes is exploring in the novel have to do with the potentially obsessive, perverse nature of love and the link between it and violence. As I said in the introductory part of this chapter, the theory that our brains are Chinese boxes containing more primitive versions of themselves could be cited to account for Graham's behaviour, which seems to be determined by forces that he cannot control rather than being freely chosen. Jack argues for a degree of freedom—and therefore of moral responsibility—when he makes the point that most people do control their violent urges, but Graham ripostes that Jack's womanizing is evidence that the novelist himself has succumbed: 'you said [that adultery is] one of the things the undeveloped part of your brain made you do. So it must have got the better of you' (76). Graham even speculates that love itself, rather than being a civilizing ideal born of our most evolved aspect, is tainted at the core by our lower natures. Jack had theorized that marriage as a social institution is responsible for the destructive emotion of jealousy, but Graham poses the following question:

> What if it wasn't something in the nature of marriage—in which case, being Jack, you could blame 'society' and then go off and be unfaithful until you felt better about it—but something in the nature of love? That was a much less pleasant thought: that the thing everyone pursued always went wrong, automatically, inevitably, chemically. (117)

What, in other words, if Graham's twisted fixation with Ann's past before she met him is not a perversion of his love for her but an extension of it? For, an obsession with the object of an individual's devotion is, notoriously, a part of the tradition of romantic love in the West, and Graham first manifests this uxorious obsessiveness about Ann in what he refers to as the 'honey time' of their relationship, even before he begins to be jealous of the on- and off-screen lovers from her past (24–5).

Barnes has said that he intended this jaundiced view that erotic love is poisoned at its roots by primitive instincts to counter the conventional belief that the social changes of the 1960s in the area of sexuality rendered it unproblematic:

> In a way it's a sort of anti-60s book. It's against the idea that somehow the 60s sorted sex out, that everyone was all fucked up beforehand, Queen Victoria was still in charge—and then along came the Beatles, suddenly everyone started sleeping with everyone else, and that cured the lot. . . . And I just wanted to say, it's not like that; that what is constant is the human heart and human passions. (McGrath 21)

As a libertine given over to displays of uninhibited, earthy, masculine physicality, Jack Lupton is the character who most embodies the spirit of sexual freedom and excess that we might associate with the 1960s. As more than one critic has noted (Abley 456; Greenwell 19), he is a perfect foil to the repressed, 'unmanly' Graham, who has lived much of his adult life in a state of detachment from his own body: 'For at least ten years he had found a diminishing use for his body; the location of all pleasure and emotion, which had once seemed to extend right to the edge of his skin, had retreated to the small space in the middle of his head' (12). The vulgar expressions with which Jack playfully spices his conversation and his penchant for farting in public are manifestations of the grotesque realism that Bakhtin locates in medieval and renaissance literature and culture and associates with 'the lower stratum of the body, the life of the belly and the reproductive organs' (*Rabelais* 21). Bakhtin champions the grotesque body as a satirical force of liberation from polite norms and abstract ideals that are out of touch with material life on earth. In his working habits as a novelist, Jack exhibits the chaotic messiness and openness to new experience that Bakhtin praises as evidence of renewal and growth (11).

However, in *Before She Met Me*, Barnes's 'anti-60s book', Jack is not positioned as a liberator. The passage from one of his novels that Graham reads exposes Jack as a bad writer, given to concocting ribald, self-aggrandizing, Harold Robbins-like fantasies of male sexual potency; the prose is purple, and the protagonist, glorified without a trace of irony, is a thinly disguised version of Jack himself. Furthermore, his counselling sessions do not free Graham from the grip of his obsession. Far from being the solution, the promiscuity that Jack represents and recommends to Graham is itself the problem. It is Graham's discovery that Jack himself has been one of Ann's former lovers that detonates Graham's explosion of violence. In Barnes's novel, unlike in Bakhtin's theory, 'the lower stratum of the body' destroys rather than enlarges our humanity. '[I]t was the offal that came out on top', thinks Graham as he travels to Repton Gardens to kill his friend. The theory that 'there were two or three different layers of the brain constantly at war with one another. . . . was only a different way of saying that your guts fucked you up, wasn't it? All it meant was that the battle-plan and the metaphor had shifted about two feet six up your body' (161). Significantly, in his frenzy Graham stabs 'repeatedly at Jack's lower body, at the area which lay between the heart and the genitals' (166).

As a novel of ideas, *Before She Met Me* also explores the same epistemological and ontological questions that I have discussed in the two previous chapters. As Pateman says, in making Graham a historian and Jack a novelist, Barnes finds a way to explore the relationship between history and fiction as narrative constructions (*Julian Barnes* 14). Pateman concludes from the increasingly deranged Graham's use of the movies in which Ann acted and Jack's fiction as sources of 'evidence' of her sexual history that Barnes invites readers to repudiate this example of 'subjectivism gone wild' ('Popularity of Ethics' 183). *Before She Met Me*, Pateman claims in the same essay, thus 'tries to reassert the truthfulness of historical events' (184). I believe, however, that Bruce Sesto is on firmer ground when he says that 'the paradox implicit in having, as central character, a historian who predicates his theoretical conclusions on cinematic "fiction" rather than on empirical "fact" embodies the contemporary novel's concern with the problematical relationship between fiction and historiography' (26). Although Graham's growing inability to separate the truth about Ann's previous relationships with men from fictional scenarios and even his own nightmares is obviously pathological, it does not follow that Barnes is implying, alternatively, that the objective truth about the past is available to us. As I stated in Chapter 3, Barnes does not deny that some matters of fact can be ascertained, and Graham does try to discover what really happened between Ann and her previous lovers: '[t]here was no point in getting jealous unless you were accurate about it; or so it seemed to Graham' (60). But the meanings of any events are dependent upon the invented narratives into which they are incorporated and the interpretations given to them. Graham's deduction that Ann had an affair with Jack is correct (although his belief that it continued even after he himself became involved with her is erroneous), but he subjectively creates the salacious narrative within which he embeds this fact: a masochistically imagined succession of couplings featuring a sexually insatiable Ann and numerous, satyr-like lovers who expose by contrast Graham's own feelings of sexual inadequacy.

Pateman is correct in saying that Graham's highly subjective reliance on fiction as an investigative tool for uncovering the reality of Ann's past is discredited by his insanity, but it is important to recognize, as Sesto does (26), that the other 'sane' characters in the novel also fictionalize history. Their phenomenological worlds are imaginative constructions. It was disconcerting to Graham, for example, that life at home with his first wife, Barbara, unlike his working experience at the university, was epistemologically ungrounded:

> With his students he could argue quite well: calmly, logically, on a basis of agreed facts. At home, there was no such basis; . . . the accusations he had to counter were a home weave of hypothesis, assertion, fantasy, and malice. Worse still was the relentless emotional overlay to the argument: the threatened price of victory might be clattering hatred, haughty silence, or a meat cleaver in the back of the head. (18–19)

It is ironic, of course, and thematically significant, that it is the seemingly rational, more civilized Graham whose final 'argument' in the ongoing debate of life is murder.

Sesto points out that Jack and Ann also fictionalize their pasts when they decide to keep from Graham the information that they once had an affair (26–7). 'I'm sorry to rewrite your past for you', Ann says to Jack, who replies, 'Don't bother, I'm always doing it myself. Every time I tell a story it's different. Can't remember how most of them started off any more. Don't know what's true. . . . Ah well, just part of the pain and pleasure of the artist's life' (67). As a novelist, Jack bases his work closely upon his life, so much so that Graham considers him unimaginative, but Jack's comment to Ann quoted above discloses the ironic fact that his life, the raw material for his fiction, is itself constituted by fictions. His very identity as a bohemian novelist is a purposeful construction, even if its various aspects do not always cohere very well. His appearance, and, frequently, his diction suggest that he is Welsh, even though he is not. Ann notices that the semiotic meaning of his attire is ambiguous: she 'had often wondered about the way Jack presented himself to the world: was he dressing down, in pursuit of a remembered or imagined yeoman simplicity; or was he dressing, in pursuit of artistic carelessness?' (65–6).

Richard Todd observes that, in his counselling sessions with Graham and Ann, Jack 'becomes a kind of surrogate novelist' (268), which I take to mean that he is a comical proxy for Barnes within the fictional world of *Before She Met Me*. A character in a novel about retrospective jealousy, Jack ironically concludes, after listening to Graham narrate his plight, that the topic is unsuitable for novelistic treatment: 'It's all a bit rarefied for me. Won't make a short story, I'm afraid' (46). Moments such as this remind us that we are, after all, reading fiction, not witnessing the unfolding of actual events. Jack's role as Barnes's surrogate is thus a means of rendering the novel self-conscious and laying bare the artifice behind its seemingly transparent realism. The implication is that fiction is everywhere. While he is giving Graham advice, Jack silently decides that the activity is very much like writing novels:

> [H]e'd been fairly convinced by the plot structure he'd presented to Graham at such short notice. He'd managed to impose some sort of pattern on both their lives as he went along. Still, that was his job, after all, wasn't it: smelting order out of chaos. . . . That was what he was paid to do, so this wasn't too hard a sideline. The percentage of lying was about the same as well. (49)

Jack's 'declared policy of living only in the present' and his 'stylized forgetting of the past' (47) might seem extreme and atypical, but it is at least viable, which is more than what can be said for Graham's deepest desire. Whereas Jack wants continually to rewrite the narrative of his own past, Graham wants to reshape time itself.

As he masochistically fantasizes about a trip to Italy that Ann once took with her then-boyfriend, he tells her, 'you . . . screwed Benny as if you would never know greater pleasure, and you . . . didn't even save a small corner of your heart and leave it untouched for when you met me' (54). How could Ann possibly change her past to prepare herself for meeting Graham in a future that she could then have known nothing about? Graham's insane desire is even more impossible than Jay Gatsby's expectation in F. Scott Fitzgerald's classic that he can repeat in the present the magical past that he once experienced with his beloved Daisy. Even though Fitzgerald diminishes the 'greatness' of Gatsby with irony, most readers experience the failure of his dream and his violent death as tragic; the bloody murder of Jack and suicide of Graham, convinced, like one of Robert Browning's mad speakers, of his own wisdom, manages only to seem shocking and bizarre.

TALKING IT OVER AND *LOVE, ETC.*

In grouping these two books within a single section, I do not mean to suggest that they are, effectively, one long novel. There are significant differences between them. The characters of *Love, etc.* are older and more disillusioned than those of *Talking It Over*. *Love, etc.*, says Michiko Kakutani, is 'an altogether darker, sourer book, a meandering saga of middle-age disappointment and regret' ('Love, Etc.' 1). It is, nevertheless, a sequel to *Talking It Over*. The two novels have common themes and share the same cast of central characters, and both feature the same narrative technique of alternating monologues spoken by the three protagonists (and by several other more peripheral characters). While the plots (or, in the terms of Russian Formalism, the *sjuzets*) of the two novels are discontinuous with one another, they imply a single, long seamless story (or *fabula*).[1] While each novel can be experienced independently of the other, a familiarity with one enriches a reading of the other.

The narrative technique of these two novels is their most striking feature. As Todd states, in dispensing with a narrator who mediates between readers and the three protagonists, Barnes employs a method of developing the narrative and disclosing the thoughts and feelings of the characters that straddles fiction and drama (275).

Stuart, Oliver, Gillian, and (less frequently) several other characters address us directly in systematically juxtaposed monologues, each one labelled with the name of the speaker. The voices are orchestrated symmetrically, and, as D. J. Taylor says, the events that they narrate are also 'painstakingly schematised and worked out' (4). In the first novel, Oliver displaces Stuart in his marriage bed with Gillian, and in the sequel Stuart undermines Oliver's position and seems to be in the process of supplanting him in his own family, at least until he loses Gillian's respect at the very end when (according to her) he rapes her. *Changing Places*, the title of one of David Lodge's campus novels, would also fit both of Barnes's books. In the sense defined by David Leon Higdon (175), both are 'chiasmic' novels that juxtapose the rising and falling fortunes of individual characters, as is Martin Amis's *Success*. In that 1977 novel, the trajectories of the two narrators reverse as the plot unfolds. Taylor (4) and other reviewers argue that Barnes was influenced by *Success* in writing *Talking It Over*, but James Buchan's charge that Barnes's work is overly derivative of and inferior to Amis's is distinctly unfair (25). The nihilistic world inhabited by Gregory Riding, Amis's dissolute representative of the upper class, and Terry Service, his loutish, working-class foster brother, feels entirely distinct from the more bourgeois social and mental space occupied by Barnes's characters. Barnes and Amis's former friendship and their common reliance on wit and other forms of verbal gymnastics notwithstanding, these are two very different writers.

Alexander Theroux remarks that Barnes's narrative method in *Talking It Over* is a variation on the epistolary novel (5),[2] but the monologues simulate speech more closely than they do writing. Indeed, early in *Love, etc.* Oliver explicitly invokes 'the privileges of the oral tradition' in order to justify his penchant for digressing (29). Vanessa Guignery draws helpfully on Bakhtin in identifying the characters' utterances as *skaz* (*Fiction* 74), one of the several types of discourse that he anatomizes in his analysis of novelistic polyphony. Bakhtin defines *skaz* as a written imitation of 'the various forms of oral everyday narration' (*Dialogic Imagination* 262). Both *Talking It Over* and *Love, etc.* are fully polyphonic in Bakhtin's terms in that none of the stylistic registers exhibited by the characters is subordinate to any other.

This sustained reliance on dramatic monologues is a departure from the more conventionally narrated *Before She Met Me*, which does feature an undramatized narrator. He exists on a separate ontological plane from the characters, and he is superior in the sense that he is psychologically omniscient with respect to their inner lives. This narrator is, however, completely detached and unobtrusive. *Before She Met Me* is like *Talking It Over* and *Love, etc.* in denying readers an authoritative, authorial perspective that adjudicates amongst contending points of view.

Necessarily, readers of *Talking It Over* and *Love, etc.* become immersed in fictional worlds within which truth, to a large degree, is relative and ambiguous. None of the characters is entirely trustworthy, as the epigraph to *Talking It Over* suggests: 'He lies like an eye-witness'. What Elaine Showalter says about *Love, etc.* holds true for the earlier novel as well: 'all three [of the protagonists] are unreliable narrators who lie to themselves as much as they lie to the reader' (3). Not everything that transpires in the two books is uncertain, of course. 'Triangulation', as Moseley says, 'is a way of achieving a rough knowledge, and the reader . . . knows with considerable accuracy who did what to whom' (137). Indeed, readers often know more than do any of the characters, a circumstance that generates much dramatic irony in both novels. For instance, when Gillian tells us in *Love, etc.* that 'Sophie's fine' (214), we know that she is ignorant of her daughter's developing bulimia. Unlike any of the other characters, we also know that Sophie's feeling that she is to blame for her father's depression is based on the erroneous belief that Stuart is her actual father and that Oliver suspects this. But some critically important facts are withheld from us. Most importantly, we simply do not know whether Stuart rapes Gillian near the conclusion of *Love, etc.*, as she claims, or whether, as he claims, they engage consensually in rough sex. As Moseley says, even when we are in possession of certain facts, judging what they mean and how to assess them morally is difficult (137). The reader's task is even more fraught when facts are in doubt.

But readers of this pair of books cannot easily choose simply to refrain from judgement because the characters are constantly soliciting it. Like Browning's dramatic monologues ('Bishop Blougram's Apology' is an example), those we encounter in *Talking It Over* and

Love, etc. frequently take the form of apologies, not usually in the sense of being acknowledgements of wrong doing, but more often in the sense of being justifications of the speakers' beliefs and deeds. As Tim Adams says, the monologues parody the confessional mode that is ubiquitous in the media culture of contemporary society, and, he also notes that in their attempts to win our sympathy the characters are like 'defence counsels for their own versions of the events' ('Eternal Triangle' 1). Erin McGraw notices that the reader's sense of participating in a judicial proceeding is enhanced by the convention that Barnes has arbitrarily adopted whereby the characters cannot talk directly to one another but can sometimes impeach the veracity of each other's statements (1–2). The three central characters draw our attention to this convention by briefly violating it in the first chapter of *Love, etc.* '[W]e have to play by the rules', Gillian eventually reminds the two men. 'No talking amongst ourselves' (8). Neither is the convention that the characters can overhear one another's monologues honoured slavishly; when they cannot, the ignorance that results produces the dramatic ironies that I discussed above.

In addressing readers in a direct, intimate fashion, Stuart, Oliver, and Gillian virtually treat us as co-characters in the two novels. Their colloquies with us go well beyond Jane Eyre's comments to the 'gentle reader' of her narrative. Barnes's trio of protagonists construct an implied reader who fully shares their reality. In introducing himself to us in *Talking It Over*, for example, Oliver 'stages' us as censorious non-smokers who reject his offer of a cigarette (10). This has the paradoxical effect of reminding us that we could not, in any event, have actually smoked the entirely non-material cigarette. The monologists' treatment of us as co-inhabitants of their fictional world, then, is a defamiliarizing, metafictional device, as Theroux observes (5). By pretending to collapse the ontological barrier that separates readers from characters, Barnes's speakers alert us to its existence. Fiction is one thing, we are reminded, and 'real life' is another. Even though the personages that we meet in novels can sometimes seem more real, intensely alive, and memorable than actual people, in an obvious respect fictional characters have no substantial reality, at least not without being actualized in the minds of readers. 'Promise not to turn your face away', Oliver implores us, and he adds a highly metafictional remark: 'if *you* decline to perceive me, then I really *shall* cease to exist' (*Talking It Over* 88).

There is a contradictory sense, however, in which treating readers as characters enhances rather than undermines realism. In this regard, Barnes has defended his decision to require readers to interact directly with his characters on the grounds that 'it's very close to how life is' (Brotton 2). 'Because the membrane between readers and characters is so thinned', he says in another interview, '[the effect] is like meeting real people' (Birnbaum, 'Interview' 5). Just as we cannot, in our day-to-day lives, depend on an intervening narrator to pronounce authoritatively on the truthfulness of what people tell us, so, in his pair of novels, we must assess the characters without any authorial assistance. Rather than estranging us from the ethical issues at stake in the novels (as a self-reflexive narrative technique might do), Barnes's method deepens our engagement, inasmuch as the characters deliberately try to make us complicit in their actions. It could even be said that, at certain moments, they try to corrupt us morally by making us identify with them as we vicariously live through their experiences. On analogy with the intentions of Camus's narrator in *La Chute* or the eponymous protagonist of Conrad's *Lord Jim*, one could argue that they try to make their auditors re-enact with them their falls from innocence to experience. At one point or another, each of the three challenges us directly to acknowledge our common guilt. Oliver, for example, badgers us to admit that we, too, have betrayed certain people in the process of forming romantic relationships with other people: 'Every love story begins with a crime. Agreed? And if we are all therefore criminals, which of us shall condemn the other? Is my case more egregious than yours?' (*Love, etc.* 14–15)

While Oliver's charge might have a certain force for some readers, his self-interested position makes his reasoning rather suspect. All of the characters' appeals to us for understanding and sympathy are vitiated to some degree by self-serving explanations and arguments—and even by outright mendacity—and this makes it difficult for readers to side unequivocally with any of them. Moreover, as the situations of the three protagonists become complicated in ways that they could not have anticipated, it becomes increasingly hard for them to believe in the values that, for them, have justified their betrayals of one another. While virtually demanding that readers become engaged ethically in the behaviour of Stuart, Oliver, and Gillian, the two novels have the overall effect of undermining many of the possible foundations for making moral judgements. In particular, as I stated in my introduction to this chapter, both *Talking It Over* and *Love, etc.* deconstruct love, the very value that all three principal characters invoke in defence of their destructive actions.

Love is positioned initially in *Talking It Over* as a potential source of meaning in a late-twentieth-century world that has been denuded of other sources of truth. 'The places where truth comes from are now less various than they used to be', says Barnes. 'Especially with the decline of the truth of religion as generally not believed anymore. The truths offered by the state seem much less reliable than they used to. And the truths of journalism are a bit hit-and-miss, as we know. And often hugely influenced by established and corporate money' (Birnbaum 'Interview' 7). None of the characters in either of the two novels has a religious faith or any other deeply sustaining structure of belief. Both Oliver and Gillian's mother, Mme Wyatt (who is presented in both novels as something of a Gallic sage), pronounce on the inherent absurdity of life in a godless universe devoid of justice. 'We are all, are we not, lost?' says Oliver. 'Those who know it not are the more lost. Those who do know it are found, for they have grasped their full lostness' (*Love, etc.* 70). In the interview quoted above, Barnes goes on to extol art as one remaining location of truth, but it is the consoling reality of love that is emphasized in *Talking It Over* and *Love, etc.*, just as it is in 'Parenthesis'. Even the most cynical characters testify to its power to infuse life with meaning and purpose.

Oliver, for example, claims to be in the broad category of people for whom love is all-encompassing: 'the purpose, the function, the bass pedal and principal melody of life' (*Talking It Over* 141). He treats love as an absolute, although he also claims, inconsistently, to be a relativist, delighting that Gillian's profession of art restoration confirms his view that objective truth is unavailable: 'Oh effulgent relativity. *There is no "real" picture under there waiting to be revealed.* What I've always said about life itself' (122). His virtual deification and worship of Gillian is a legacy of the medieval tradition of *amour courtois*: 'Loaves and fishes. I bet Stuart sees her basically as a good little shopper. Whereas for me she works miracles' (114). The miracle in question, also a vestige of courtly love, is his own moral and psychological transformation: 'I want to lay my life before [Gillian], don't you see? I'm starting over, I'm clean, I'm *tabula rasa*' (142). Even Stuart, who tends to see personal identity as much more stable and fixed than does Oliver, with his Wildean program of self-fashioning, believes that Gillian has worked magic on him: 'I've stayed the same as I was before but now it's all right to be what I was before. The princess kissed the frog and he didn't turn into a handsome prince but that was all right because she liked him as a frog' (55). What Gillian has transformed in fairy-tale fashion is not his identity but his former feelings about its lack of worth. For all her practicality, Gillian, too, is, in the words of Sven Birkerts, 'one of love's great susceptibles' (3). She has a Laurentian sensitivity to the primal, seemingly mystical erotic connection that cuts through the quotidian social aspect of life. She is open to 'that moment when someone is suddenly there, and says, without using the words, "It's me. It's you. That's all there is to say." As if some vast truth is being guessed at before your eyes, and all you have to do is reply, "Yes, I think it's true, too"' (*Love, etc.* 189–90).

It is paradoxical, to say the least, that in treating love as their central value and motive force, Stuart, Oliver, and Gillian inflict severe pain on each other that they then try to justify ethically by invoking the very love responsible for that damage. If love really is the source of what is beneficial in life, we might ask, why does it wreak such havoc? Should we accept their claims that the overmastering power of love exonerates them from responsibility for their actions? 'I'd probably be a bit dubious in your position', Gillian tells the reader in *Talking It Over*, '[b]ut I'd just like to say this. I didn't choose what happened . . . It happened to me. I married Stuart, then I fell in love with Oliver' (179). Oliver, similarly, pleads that 'I had no choice, not really. No-one ever does, not without being a completely different person' (196). Living in an unmythical age, the characters do not invoke Cupid and his arrows, but readers familiar with the Petrarchan tradition of love will have no difficulty in making the connection. The medieval church impugned the cult of erotic love on moral grounds, and readers of Barnes's novels might similarly ask, as Stuart finally does, whether love really does transform people for the better, if in the process it deprives them of free will and responsibility for their behaviour: 'who ever said that love makes us better people, or makes us behave better? Whoever said that?' (*Love, etc.* 158). Stuart's long-enduring love for Gillian, then, cannot justify the cruel revenge that he takes (without fully admitting to himself that he is doing it) upon Oliver in *Love, etc.* and the unhappiness that Oliver's family members experience as a result of his paralysing depression. The two novels imply that love is not so much the foundation for ethical behaviour as a capricious, uncontrollable force that is ungoverned morally. 'Maman, I thought there were *rules*' (*Talking It Over* 169), Gillian cries, after discovering to her horror that love is unregulated, not bound by the institution of marriage in a way that will keep her safe from danger. 'It is always the dangerous time', her mother tells her (147).

Having treated love as a stable foundation for their lives, Stuart, Oliver, and Gillian find that love does not endure unchanged. By the conclusion of *Love, etc.*, it seems to have died altogether, or at least to have mutated unrecognizably. Of course, the dramatically shifting nature of love is the very stuff from which narratives featuring erotic triangles, such as Barnes's two, are crafted. Oliver's attempt in *Talking It Over* to explain and justify the transfer of Gillian's affections from Stuart to him contextualizes love so as to emphasize its instability and precarious reality. Since Stuart is a banker, Oliver makes a parallel between love and money, which fluctuates in value according to market forces: '[Love and money] both go where they wist, reckless of what they leave behind. Love too has its buyouts, its asset stripping, its junk bonds. Love rises and falls in value like any currency. And confidence is *such* a key to maintaining its value' (160).

At first Stuart resists the bleak implications of Oliver's fanciful analogy: that love, lacking any intrinsic value or reality, is relative, circumstantial, and contingent; and that Gillian is simply a possession or commodity to be passed between the men.[3] 'We're not talking about money, we're talking about love', he tells Oliver. But Stuart comes to accept fully that love 'is only what people agree exists, what they agree to put a notional value on. . . . If you ask me, I think love is trading artificially high. One of these days the bottom is going to fall out of love' (*Talking It Over* 233). Even before his marriage to Gillian disintegrates Oliver concurs prophetically: 'Imagine that: the death of love. It could happen' (222). As Pateman says, Oliver's and Stuart's cynical line of thought represents 'the complete immersal of the discourse of love into the discourse of commerce'. Pateman concludes that the 'effect of this is to alter the nature of love' (*Julian Barnes* 58), but clearly the pair believe that they have revealed, rather than altered, the already- and always-illusory nature of love.

The way in which *Love, etc.* concludes bears out this pessimism about love, which drains from Oliver and Gillian's marriage like water from a leaky pail. '[I]f . . . money may be compared to love', Oliver says near the end of *Talking It Over*, 'then marriage is the bill. I jest. I half-jest, anyway' (249). Brooding over the fact that she no longer tells Oliver that she loves him, Gillian thinks, 'It's my children who bring out the "I" in "I love you." Do "I" still love Oliver? Yes, "I" think so, "I" suppose so. You could say that I'm managing love' (*Love, etc.* 146). But she is unable to manage even the tepid love connecting her to Oliver, because by the end of *Love, etc.*, after he has learned that she deceived him when they lived in France by deliberately provoking his violence so that Stuart could witness it, he exclaims bitterly that 'all relationships . . . are about power. . . . and the sources of power are so old, so familiar, so cruelly deterministic, so simple, that they have but simple names. Money, beauty, talent, youth, age, love, sex, strength, money, more money, yet more money' (193–4). Oliver knows that Gillian has resented his impecuniousness and that Stuart has used financial generosity in an attempt to regain her favour, but, ironically, Stuart's love falters just when he thinks that he might have won her back:

> The sex didn't make things clearer. On the contrary, it made me realize I've been deceiving myself by assuming . . . that I've always loved Gill, always have and always will. . . . Now that it seems there's an outside chance of getting back what I once had, part of me is beginning to wonder how much I want it. (226)

There is dramatic irony here, for we know that Gillian has lost what respect she had for him because she thinks that he raped her. Did Stuart really want to regain her love, we might ask, or did he harbour an unacknowledged desire to avenge himself upon her as well as upon Oliver? Why else would he rape her, if rape her he did?

And, finally, what is the status of the one ostensibly selfless act of love apparent in the two novels: the domestic violence engineered by Gillian for Stuart's benefit? Pateman exalts this event as 'that attempt at reparation, that attempt to find an idiom that withstands and flaunts contingency and terror, that is the sign of love' (61). The problem with Pateman's reading, of course, is that Barnes renders Gillian's intended act of caritas wholly ironic in its effects. Early in *Love, etc.*, Stuart confides that what he witnessed in France 'didn't help' (12), and when he learns that Gillian stage-managed the entire scene, he feels deeply betrayed, just as Oliver does. Gillian laments, 'It didn't work, did it? Ten years ago, I engineered a scene which I thought would set Stuart free. But it seems to have had the opposite effect' (223). At the novel's end, with Gillian pregnant from her sexual encounter with Stuart, there seems little to nourish the growth of more love in the lives of the three principals. Mme Wyatt's concluding thoughts, which would not be out of place in a play by Beckett, are fittingly dour: 'Something will happen. Or nothing. And then, one after another, over a long period of time, we'll all die. You may die first, of course' (227).

6

STARING AT THE SUN AND
THE PORCUPINE

METAPHYSICS AND POLITICS

The fourth of Barnes's novels to be published under his own name, *Staring at the Sun* is philosophical in character, whereas his seventh, *The Porcupine*, focuses on politics. The former narrates the life story of an ordinary woman and, in the process, explores metaphysical dilemmas that have gripped humans perennially, while the latter novel is a courtroom drama that exposes the political turmoil ensuing from the transformation of an unnamed Balkan country (based primarily on Bulgaria) from communism to democracy and a market economy. What the two books have in common is a postmodernist, anti-foundationalist orientation on the philosophical and political issues with which their characters wrestle. *Staring at the Sun*'s Jean Serjeant and her son Gregory find no authoritative answers to the myriad questions that they pose about such matters as whether life has any inherent meaning, whether death is final, and whether God exists; and *The Porcupine*'s Peter Solinsky finds in his successful prosecution of Stoyo Petkanov, the former communist dictator, no clear evidence that the switch from tyranny to democracy and freedom has served the higher causes of truth, justice and social progress. Both novels suggest that any solutions

122

to the large, recurrent problems that beset individuals or societies at large will be ambiguous and contingent, lacking in finality and legitimacy.

As he does in his other novels, in both *Staring at the Sun* and *The Porcupine* Barnes interrogates the role of language in the social construction of meaning, showing how even honest attempts to disclose reality in words are complicated and undercut by the circuitous, treacherous processes of linguistic systems. If Barnes does not suggest that language is completely decentred, he certainly implies that it operates at an oblique angle to its referents. Applied in thought, language proves to be as unreliable and imprecise an epistemological tool as memory. Easily rigidified into conventional formulae and jargons, language serves in both novels as an ideological instrument of social control that is more likely to obscure truth than to reveal it. In *Staring at the Sun*, for example, the most difficult barrier in Jean's struggle to free herself from her oppressive, stifling marriage to Michael is the discursive prison of platitudes meant to reconcile women to their own subjugation in a patriarchal society: 'Stick it out; rough with the smooth; devil you know; ups and downs; can't last forever. How often had she heard such phrases, cheerfully delivered and cheerfully believed? Running away, people said, showed a lack of courage' (80). 'The Porcupine', Nick Hornby rightly says, 'is as much about the inadequacy of political language as it is about political turmoil' ('Much Matter' 11). Readers of the novel quickly see that the defeat of communism has not put an end to evasive uses of language. As Guignery says, its 'totalitarian and imprisoning ideology is . . . reflected in a sterilised, stilted and uniform language which still prevails' (*Fiction* 93). It appears in a memorandum read by Peter Solinsky, who 'discard[s] the jargon automatically. . . . That was one of the few skills you learnt under Socialism: the ability to filter out bureaucratic distortions of language' (*Porcupine* 91). While the new régime does begin to jettison the elaborately evolved argot of communism, it quickly develops new euphemisms and dissimulations of its own. Both *Staring at the Sun* and *The Porcupine* manifest the tension that is discernible in all of Barnes's fiction between a need to discover and bear witness to fundamental truths about life and a worry that they can be apprehended only subjectively and expressed in words only inadequately.

STARING AT THE SUN

Staring at the Sun is similar in some obvious respects to *England, England*. Both novels have female protagonists whose extraordinary longevity enables them to live through momentous historical changes. The lives of both Jean Serjeant and Martha Cochrane extend from different points in the twentieth century into a twenty-first-century future beyond the time in which Barnes wrote the books. He was therefore able to project worrisome aspects of contemporary society into a dystopian vision of a Britain deformed by applications of electronic technology. In *England, England*, these technologies enable the creation of a malign virtual reality on the Isle of Wight, and in *Staring at the Sun* the state employs a supercomputer—which boasts a function labelled The Absolute Truth (TAT)—in order to pacify and control citizens by usurping their capacity to cogitate, speculate, and imagine. As Pateman explains (*Julian Barnes* 39, 74–5), both novels also have in common tripartite narrative structures, the individual parts of which do not bond together into totalizing wholes. Those parts are, as Pateman says, 'generically discrete' (35). The novels incorporate elements of the *bildungsroman*, historical fiction, political satire, and futuristic, speculative fiction. This generic hybridism produces a certain amount of tension and contradiction, because readers are denied the ability to activate one consistent set of codes with which to interpret the novels. We are thus reminded that no one kind of narrative report is natural, complete, and authoritative. What Pateman says of *Staring at the Sun* applies to both novels: 'By placing . . . social narratives that promise closure within a heterogeneous play of genres that discourage closure, the novel seems to tend toward a "postmodern" notion of a knowledge that prioritizes heterogeneity, dissensus, and openness' (39). Since he celebrates *Staring at the Sun* for this dialogic mixing of genres, it is surprising to me that Pateman castigates this same feature of *England, England* as an artistic weakness (75), just as it is surprising that David Lodge, who has himself violated generic boundaries in some of his heavily postmodernist fictions, criticizes *Staring at the Sun* for lacking organic unity. After usefully drawing on the work of Bakhtin to label both *Flaubert's Parrot* and *Staring at the Sun* as Menippean satires (the distinguishing characteristics of which are ' "philosophical invention", "sharp contrasts and oxymoronic combinations", and "a wide use of inserted genres" '), Lodge then complains that the latter novel is 'a broken-backed whole, a book that starts out as one thing and ends up as another' ('Home Front' 21). He illogically demands the sort of unity that Menippean satire lacks, according to the very definition of it that he offers.

The first section of *Staring at the Sun* opens on Jean as a nonagenarian looking back, through the precarious lenses of memory, at her life as a small child in the 1930s. The focus of the narration is her perplexity in the face of life's many enigmas and her search for answers. As Guignery says (*Fiction* 57), the epigraph to this section, taken from a letter written by Chekhov, adumbrates the futility of her long quest for life's hidden meanings: 'You ask me what life is? It is like asking what a carrot is. A carrot is a carrot, and nothing more is known.' Part and parcel of Jean's questioning is her need to discover what sorts of fulfilment are available to her as a human being. The brief prologue to the novel describing the oxymoronic 'ordinary miracle' witnessed by Tommie Prosser in the cockpit of his Hurricane during the Second World War—the sun rising twice in the same morning—suggests that wondrous experiences are possible, but the earliest memory that Jean recounts conveys metaphorically the conflicting message that her life will be barren of satisfactions. Her favourite uncle Leslie's gift to her of hyacinths just beginning to grow in a pot covered over with brown paper proves in the spring when she unwraps it to be a dead crop of golf tees planted upside down in the soil. As the novel unfolds, however, Jean comes to experience what Carlos Fuentes refers to as 'enchantment[s]' to counterbalance the many 'disenchantment[s]' that begin with Leslie's mean practical joke (1). As a person, Jean is unexceptional, but, as Moseley states, her story nevertheless encompasses 'the extraordinary that lies just beneath or beyond the ordinary' (101).

In Jean's search for understanding and fulfilment, she depends for guidance upon male authority figures, whom she must ultimately reject. As Fuentes observes, she comes to see that she must 'create her own circle of enchantment' (2). The first man who holds out the promise of something special is Leslie, one of those adults to whom children are drawn because they can enter into the imaginative space of children. Moseley says that for Jean Leslie is 'one of the people connected with the mysterious, or the numinous, or the uncanny' (101), but it is important to recognize that this connection is more apparent than real. Jean eventually rejects his magic, which is all sleight of hand and trickery. '[P]erhaps she had grown out of Uncle Leslie', she thinks to herself as a middle-aged woman (83).

Unlike Jean, who as a child is the victim of dramatic irony, readers can see from the beginning that Leslie is a comic-ironic demiurge, not the legitimate creator of wonder. Adult readers recognize him as a stereotypical figure of the 1930s, the roguish, anti-Semitic, golf-loving sportsman who is attracted to fascism and who speaks in schoolboy slang of the day. For Jean, this only dimly understood code holds out the promise of an alternative, enhanced reality, but readers see that his hyperbolic terminology is purely conventional in nature. His 'Old Green Heaven' is just a golf course; badly hit shots in its bunkers do not really send 'more sand flying than on a windy day in the Gobi desert' (9). His slang holds no buried truths for Jean to understand later, just misinformation, stock ideas, and prejudices:

> At the fifth [hole] he told her that tomatoes were the cause of cancer, and that the sun would never set on the empire; at the tenth she learned that bombers were the future, and that old Musso might be an Eytie but he knew which way the paper folded. (10)

Far from being a figure of authority, Leslie is, as he later confesses to Jean, a life-long coward (130). His existential terror is expressed in the secret screaming game that they play on the golf course, where they roar 'at the empty heavens, knowing that however much noise [they] made, nobody up there would hear [them]' (159). Unlike his confident slang, which implicitly suggests a mastery of the world around him that he cannot really exert, his screams of protest at the sky are inarticulate. He has no language with the power to fill the emptiness of the universe that surrounds him.

In a novel in which, according to Barnes himself, one of the themes is the nature of heroism, another compromised male guide for Jean is Prosser, of whom Barnes says that he 'isn't a hero with a mustache and a Spitfire who shoots down Germans. He's someone who's sort of cracked and eventually kills himself' (Smith 74). When after the war Jean visits Prosser's widow, she tells Jean that 'I always thought he had a bit of a yellow streak in him myself' (103). Nevertheless, it is Prosser who initiates Jean into the mysteries of flight, which, as several critics have indicated, is a metaphoric leitmotif in the novel (Hennegan 39; Hulbert 38; Moseley 105). For Alison Hennegan, flight is 'many-meaninged: soaring aspiration, cowardly retreat, necessary escape, a defiance of nature explicable by natural laws' (39); for Moseley, flight signifies 'a way of transcendence' (106). As a symbol, then, flight is ambiguous, as is Prosser as a mentor. For Jean, who tends to defend him, he is not self-evidently guilty of cowardice, since its opposite, bravery has only a nebulous reality. '"I can't tell you what it's like being brave", Prosser tells her. "You can't pick it up and look at it. When it's there you don't feel it's there.... You can't talk about it. It isn't there"' (49). Does his committing suicide by flying towards the sun until he has lost consciousness represent a craven violation of moral law, or a courageous choice to die on his own terms? For the reader, there is no clear answer, but it is good to remember what Jean thinks when Prosser first tells her about his plan: 'You couldn't very well say it all sounded brave and beautiful to you, even if that was exactly what it did sound like' (32).

Her father and her husband are two representatives of patriarchy whom Jean must throw off in her pursuit of individuation and fulfilment. Both preside over a seemingly immutable, benign natural order of things that proves for Jean to be both inessential and oppressive. As Guignery says, the 'figures of authority are . . . masculine and deny any possibility of contradiction or uncertainty, as epitomized by Jean's father' (57). He is a man who has taken his sense of personal identity from his social function, so that the inner and outer men are seemingly in perfect accord:

> Her father, who managed the grocery at Bryden, looked like a man who managed a grocery: he was round and neat, hitched up his sleeves with a pair of elasticated steel bands, and seemed as if he was kind but had a reserve of severity—the sort of man who knew that a pound of flour was a pound of flour and not fifteen ounces. (20–1)

He experiences none of Jean's befuddlement in the face of life's mysteries not only because he is a mature adult while she is just a child but also, more importantly, because for him the restrictive ideology of his social class and his nation provides a sufficient definition of reality.

As a policeman, Jean's husband, Michael, symbolically enforces the masculine order that subordinates her as a woman and restricts her to the domestic sphere. As Lodge says, Barnes's treatment of her dilemma suggests that he is 'contemplating, with a consciousness raised by the feminism of the 1970s, the plight of women in the 1940s, caught up in a war generated and managed by men' (21). Michael uses the authority conferred upon him during the war to ensure that blackout curtains are in place in private homes as a pretext for meeting her. Initially, he behaves like Leslie in that he tries to capture her interest with a trick, crossing his legs under a long coat to make it look as though his feet have been reversed. Like Leslie's, the magic that he creates for her is really just illusion; his soon-to-be-declared love will not really constitute a transcendent reality that can enlighten her and fulfil her needs as a person. Until her disillusionment, however, she conceives of him as 'the answer, whatever might have been the question' (38). Despite some hesitancy, Jean embraces the romance plot culminating in marriage as the process by which her full selfhood as a woman will be realized and by which she will gain the knowledge of life that she has been seeking.

Jean's first dissatisfaction as a newly married woman comes in the very sphere in which she expects gratification and delight: that of sexuality. Like her other ideas about love and marriage, her expectations concerning sex are conditioned by narratives that transmit the ideology of patriarchy. Because she has been told that '[m]en were supposed to know' (40), she assumes, quite erroneously, that Michael will be able to instruct her sexually: 'Of course she loved him, of course it would be all right; of course he would know everything.... It would be beautiful; it might even be spiritual, as some people said' (56). Her only source of information is a book written by a female sexologist. Finding the prose by turns obscurely technical and clinical on the one hand and euphemistically high-flown and romantic on the other, Jean soon decides that 'the book...was clearly rubbish' (43). Its language proves to be wholly detached from the actuality of Jean's eventual experience in bed with Michael, who, before their marriage is consummated, enlists another female 'expert', an intimidating gynaecologist, to 'inspect' her and train her in the use of a diaphragm. Thoroughly demoralized and afraid, Jean is ill-prepared for physical intimacy with a man who is ignorant of women's sexual needs. Far from being an ecstatic revelation of one of life's great truths, having sex with Michael is distinctly anti-climactic for her. At best, she experiences a mild sort of pleasure that she likens to the shoelace game that she played as a child with Leslie: 'That's what it was like: ticklish, and nice, and a bit funny, and different' (64).[1]

Rather than opening up a rewarding future for Jean as a human being, marriage closes it off. 'Getting married was an end, not a beginning', she thinks not long after her wedding (64). Pateman is correct to conclude on the basis of Jean's 20 years with Michael that '[m]arriage as an answer, as a social narrative, as a closed genre of discourse, is seen to be stultifying, degenerative, and dangerous for the individual who prioritizes it' (Pateman, *Julian Barnes* 37). Like so many of the uses of language examined in *Staring at the Sun*, the discourses of marriage are internally consistent but largely ungrounded. Yearning for a first-rate life, Jean analyses the deficiencies of her second-rate married life so as to emphasize the disconnection between what her and Michael's words signify and the reality of their emotional lives:

> You had to obey certain rules, permit certain angers, respect certain forms of lying; you had to appeal to feelings in the other person which both of you pretended were there even if you suspected they weren't. This, of course, was part of what she meant by a second-rate life. (77)

For Barnes, and for his creation Jean, the nature of a first-rate life is not self-evident, and therefore her goal is not accomplished simply by fleeing her suffocating marriage. In rejecting the established social authority and order of the nuclear family, Jean sets out on an open-ended quest for meaning. There is no clearly defined alternative to her life with Michael that promises fulfilment. She is driven by no great ambition, no sense of religious or political mission. Had she been of a different generation, the cause of feminism might have enlisted her, as it does Gregory's girlfriend, the angry, man-hating Rachel, who seems something of a stereotype, despite Barnes's claim that she is 'drawn from life' and 'done very realistically' (McGrath 22). It is true that Jean leaves as a new mother, who values her baby as 'an ordinary miracle' (81), but, as Hennegan states, she does not derive a complete sense of identity from being a mother or from any other role: 'Jean eludes definition as wife, mother, widow. The experiences shape her life but do not contain its essence' (38). For most of her life, Jean carries a thin strip of tin with her maiden name embossed upon it not because she has a firm sense of who she is but because she needs to counteract a precarious sense of selfhood. After all, she first acquires the strip as a defensive reaction just before her name and her identity are about to be changed with her marriage.

Jean's search for a significant life becomes literalized as physical journeys to the locales that she takes to be the Seven Wonders of the World. 'Maybe anyone could make up their own private seven', she thinks. 'Why not?' (89) This subjectivity and the fact that she travels to the sites alone are indications that for Barnes important truths cannot be institutionalized, packaged, or determined by social consensus. It is a trip to the Grand Canyon—the lone natural, as opposed to human-made, wonder—that occasions an epiphany for her. The Canyon acts upon her as a magnificent, vast, natural edifice open to the sky, and the reality that it communicates to her is similarly unbounded conceptually. The narrator compares the Canyon to Europe's great Gothic cathedrals, but its effect is not to reveal God to her, or even anything at all that is definite: 'Perhaps the Canyon acted like a cathedral on religiously inclined tourists and startlingly argued without words the power of God and the majesty of his works. Jean's response was the opposite. The Canyon stunned her into uncertainty'. Whatever its reality, it impresses her as 'a place beyond words, beyond human noise, beyond interpretation' (100). Like Prosser's extraordinary sight over the English Channel, her visual experience at the Canyon involves both the sun and an aeroplane flying. As Moseley says, that she looks down on the plane from above is 'a sort of miracle' (102). Like Prosser's, however, her 'miracle' is natural and this-worldly, not transcendent or supernatural: 'We [say] "against nature" when we [mean] "against reason." It [is] nature which [provides] the miracles, the hallucinations, the beautiful trickery' (101).

In the third part of the novel, the timid, spectatorial Gregory's quest for meaning takes the form not of adventurous travel but

of sedentary, anguished philosophical exploration of basic problems that have plagued humans for millennia. His questioning
and cogitation produce results that are neither exactly fruitless
nor especially conclusive. While he ultimately rejects suicide and
affirms the value of life, he finds no definitive answers to his questions about its purpose, the nature of courage, the characteristics
of a good life and a good death, the possibility of God's existence,
and the character of God (if he does indeed exist) and the nature of
his relationship to human beings. In fact, Gregory concludes that
thought is finally pointless:

> Question and answer, question and answer, question and answer—
> listen to the rattle of the human brain, driving back and forth like an
> industrial loom. . . . Finally you realized that question and answer were
> the same, that the one enclosed the other. Stop the loom, the futile
> chattering loom of human thought. (191)

In the final stages of his search, he seeks the counsel of his
mother, who effectively supplants the monologic authority of TAT
and the Orwellian General Purposes Computer, which he had
been consulting regularly.[2] Gregory thus resists totalitarian pressures masquerading as democracy, just as his mother had with-
stood social conditioning before him in rejecting the ideology
that bound her, against her own instincts, to her husband. For
all her wisdom, Jean, as Gregory knows, really has no access
to absolute truth, and the answers that she gives to his questions about death, religion, and suicide convey a certainty that
she really does not feel. Consequently, her advice does not really
become an ontological grounding that would discredit Pateman's
identification of the novel's position on knowledge as postmodern (Pateman, *Julian Barnes* 39). Nevertheless, it is fair to say that
Staring at the Sun comes close to discounting the reality of an oth-
erworldly, supernatural dimension. Both mother and son believe
in the existence of a soul that outlives the body, but they arrive
independently of each other at the conclusion that the soul is
neither immortal nor transcendent. 'The sky *is* the limit', Jean
tells Gregory, as they set off together in the novel's concluding scene for a flight in an aeroplane. 'Yes, Mother' (195), he
replies.

THE PORCUPINE

Reviewers were quick to notice that *The Porcupine* is unique amongst Barnes's novels in being directly concerned with politics (Bayley 30; Puddington 62), although, as I have already discussed in this study, most of the fictions that he wrote before and after *The Porcupine* are also political (at least in a broad sense) in revealing how power functions discursively in societies in the form of ideologies. This novel reveals the same interest in the struggle of women that is expressed in *Staring at the Sun*. The new liberal democratic régime has, apparently, not entirely eradicated the pervasive sexism of the previous communist one, for the novel opens with housewives protesting the shortages that have plagued the country's transition to a market economy. Their disenfranchisement is indicated in the fact that their demonstration is wordless, if not actually silent (they bang pots and other kitchen implements, which in itself indicates symbolically their restriction to the private, domestic sphere). As Guignery says (*Fiction* 93–4), they distrust language, since it has been debased and rendered treacherous by the communists. And these politically marginalized women obviously have no access to any new linguistic formulations that command power in their changed society. Still, as Petkanov tells Solinsky, under the old régime there would have been no protest of any kind: 'A government that cannot keep its women in the kitchen is fucked, Solinsky, fucked' (*Porcupine* 13).

John Bayley labels Barnes's treatment of politics in *The Porcupine* 'committed' (30), but Moseley properly rejects this designation, since, as he says, the novel does not self-evidently present the political issues in a partisan fashion (149). As I said in the introductory part of this chapter, Barnes's treatment of the conflict between representatives of the old and new governments emphasizes the absence of absolute or even firm standards for adjudicating these debates. The old political system was tyrannical and corrupt, but its successor is inept and, perhaps, equally corrupt. Despite Solinsky's extolling of freedom and truth, the movement of which he is a part is afflicted with a cynicism like what Barnes heard described as 'the death of idealism' during his first visit to Bulgaria ('Candles for the Living' 7). The people might have been oppressed under communism, but they were given what Petkanov calls 'higher things' (*The Porcupine* 105), as well as the basic material necessities of life. In contrast, the 'Changes' seem to offer only 'the chill embrace of the Market' ('Candles for the Living' 7). As Childs says, however, 'Barnes is in no wise a simple reactionary but is predisposed to see the arguments on both sides' (84). Barnes himself refers to *The Porcupine* as

> a political novel about that old but still true problem: the weakness of liberalism confronted by the certainty of a system that believes it has all the answers. And this is still the case even when liberalism has triumphed. It's still the case that though the dictator, the man with an answer for everything, is put on trial and found guilty, in a way he's the victor. (Freiburg 61)

The book should not be classified as a satire, Barnes argues in the same interview, because there is no clear object of attack; it is impossible, therefore, to tell who or what is being satirized.[3] He agrees with his interviewer that satire is no longer viable because widely shared belief in the norms upon which it depends has waned (Freiburg 61).

The Porcupine's treatment of its subject matter, then, is postmodernist, even though its formal structure is (uncharacteristically for Barnes) highly conventional, as critics have observed (Moseley 148; Pateman, *Julian Barnes* 63). In the absence of agreed upon, universal standards, the proposal for a 'moral trial' that the State contemplates for Petkanov is rejected. This context of uncertainty and relativity troubles a citizenry hungry for truth and justice. For example, Vera—a member of the group of students who watch the trial of Petkanov unfold on television and comment, in choric fashion, upon it—initially trusts that the country's political metamorphosis will produce 'the end of lies and illusions; now the time had arrived when truth was possible' (20). And Solinksy, 'who prefer[s] facts to ideology, who wants to establish small truths before proceeding to the larger ones' (27), intends the trial to be honest and fair. The government office that appointed him Prosecutor stressed 'that correct judicial procedures must be followed. The days were gone of laying a broad charge which could then be interpreted by the court as covering whatever behaviour the State decided to punish' (38). But, conflictingly, everyone involved officially in the trial knows 'that anything other than a verdict of guilty [is] unacceptable to higher authority'. Consequently, '[r]ules of evidence and questions of admissibility [are] broadly interpreted' (58). In the end, lacking hard evidence linking Petkanov to the monstrous crimes against humanity that he is commonly believed to have committed and forced to try him only for trivial offences under the dubious laws in place during his Communist dictatorship, Solinsky perverts justice when he brandishes a document that he suspects to be forged and accuses Petkanov of having murdered his own daughter. Pateman perfectly captures the absurdly tautological character of Solinsky's melodramatic gambit: 'fakes, forgeries, and lies are the platforms for a justice that is supposed to be condemning fakes, forgeries, and lies' (66).

The trial degenerates, as Yonka Krasteva argues, into a species of postmodern spectacle rather than an honest attempt to locate the elusive truths about the crimes of the old régime:

> [T]he novel is about the staging of a spectacle with a definite script which is irritatingly modified by the refusal of the accused to cooperate with his accusers. The narrative itself runs like a film, a film about the preparation of the trial, conversations behind the scenes, the trial itself. The TV viewers who provide commentaries all the time . . . are another indication that we are in the postmodern world where representation and act are inseparable. What we have become accustomed to accepting as 'reality' acquires a fictitious, film-like, two-dimensional quality where image is everything. (347)

There is nothing naïve about Petkanov's uncooperativeness; he is a media-savvy public person, who plays expertly to the cameras and who fully expects his enemies to 'stage the trial their way, how it suited them, lying and cheating and fixing evidence' (17). His method of defending himself is not to counter the showy unreality of the trial with unvarnished facts but, like an accomplished actor, to steal scenes and sway public opinion by creating theatrical impressions that cast him in a heroic light. Guignery astutely notes that he is 'suspicious of the retrievability of truth and views the trial in dramatic terms' (91).

Petkanov's cynicism about the trial and slipperiness under questioning do not mean that he is in any doubt about the ultimate rightness of either his political thinking or his performance over 33 years as party leader and head of state. His Marxist epistemology gives him what he believes to be an absolute scientific scale of judgement, a solid foundational authority for his views and actions. He believes that the fall of the Soviet empire and his own overthrow marks only the loss of a battle, not of the ongoing war between progressive socialists and bourgeois, counter-revolutionary fascists. 'What [i]s happening', thinks Petkanov,

> [i]s that just for a brief historical moment the old system [is] being allowed a last little hop in its slimy frog-pond. But then, inevitably, the spirit of Socialism will shake itself again, and in *our* next jump we shall squelch the capitalists down into the mud until they expire beneath our boots. (114–15)

He believes that the Court of History will exonerate him and his comrades and will convict their persecutors, just as some of his most ardent opponents, such as Vera, think that the defeat of his party is the objective judgement of history upon it: 'They had to be witnesses, Vera insisted. All four of them together: Vera, Atanas, Stefan, and Dimiter. This was a great moment in their country's history' (19–20).

For Barnes, however, as I argued in Chapter 4, there is no monolithic, totalizing History with a capital letter that objectively records its own unassailable judgements. There are only plural, sometimes competing, humanly created histories, which are fraught in all sorts of ways. Guignery is accurate in her claim that '*The Porcupine*, like *A History of the World in 10¹/₂ Chapters*, conveys an equal suspicion of the master narratives of Communism and capitalism, or an "incredulity towards metanarratives," to repeat Jean-François Lyotard's quote' (*Fiction* 95).[4] Unlike his character Petkanov, Barnes has no belief in a historicism that enables him to predict the future course of events. Accordingly, as several commentators have said, his narrative in *The Porcupine* ends ambiguously, without closure (Lázaro 125; Pateman, *Julian Barnes* 70; Sesto 122).

Barnes's postmodernist orientation is also shown in the way in which historical fact and invented fiction are combined in the novel. As both Sesto (125) and Guignery (*Fiction* 88) have pointed out, in addition to being violated within the world of the novel, the boundaries between these two ontological realms were points of controversy in the novel's reception in Bulgaria. Barnes himself wrote on this subject in a brief essay about visiting that country to promote the book, which was first published in Bulgarian, not in English: 'There were certainly problems over the demarcation line between fiction and reality. Some complained that my dictator was more intelligent than theirs had been; others wanted to correct what they saw as factual errors' ('Stranger than Fiction' 140). Yet some Bulgarian readers, such as the Prosecutor upon whom Solinsky was based, praised Barnes's prescient insight into the deposed Todor Zhivkov (on whom Petkanov is partially modelled): 'He asked how I'd known various details of Zhivkov's behind-the-scenes behaviour; I answered (using the novelist's technical term), "I guessed"' (140). It would seem from Barnes's report here that his synthesis of real-world and made-up characters has had contradictory effects on readers. As I suggested while discussing *Flaubert's Parrot*, and as Sesto says with reference to *The Porcupine* (126), the mixing of characters based upon historical personages with entirely or largely fictional ones both enhances verisimilitude and works in an opposite fashion as an alienating device to puncture the illusion of reality, thereby implying that all discursive representations of experience have a large imaginary dimension.

Barnes's rejection of the claim that narratives can reflect reality in an objective, unitary fashion is revealed in his handling of points of view in the novel. There is no single, privileged vantage from which truth might be glimpsed in the novel. It is true, as Lázaro indicates, that the narrator has a godlike psychological and spatial omniscience regarding the characters, but he does not preside like a judge or an editorialist over his fictional world (128). His detachment, like that of Barnes's other undramatized narrators, amounts to a refusal to instruct readers how to interpret the text's meanings. Although Barnes has been criticized for presuming, without an intimate knowledge of their culture or history, to give unmediated access into the inner lives of eastern Europeans (Bayley 32; Scammell 4), his narrator does not set himself up as their superior in understanding. On the contrary, he effaces himself so completely that he does not even constitute one of the many points of view that contend for our attention in the novel. All of these perspectives are limited and fallible. Relativity prevails. Even the chorus of students do not speak with one voice, as though they could express the unified opinions of the populace. Instead, they frequently wrangle and disagree vehemently with one another.

The dialogic welter of voices and opinions that swelled after the fall of the old régime does not satisfy the need that many people have for certainty and direction in life. Barnes speculates that this craving accounts for the interest that he witnessed in Bulgaria in 'esoteric cults' and practises such as numerology and astrology: 'When one closed system of thought fails, the intellectually giddying prospect of relativity makes other explain-it-all cults attractive. Even the Moonies have arrived with their version of the Total Answer' ('Candles for the Living' 6). However, despite the anxiety and confusion that it can generate, the dialogue has some salutary effects. Under the monologic discourse of communism, censorship prevailed. With free speech, those who are oppressed or marginalized in society have at least the possibility of voicing their protests. Pateman cautions, though, that '[a]ccess to the multiplicity of language games that comes with the defeat of Communism is not a guarantee of any greater justice' (69), and the injustice of the theatrical 'show' trial around which the novel's plot revolves certainly suggests that he is right.

However, the success of the student-run Devinsky Commando in directly challenging the power of the army during a demonstration against the old communist régime shows that verbal protest can in some circumstances lead to real political change. Their ironic displays, which Sesto identifies as carnivalesque in nature (126), disclose the corruption and mendacity of both the old and new governments beneath their poses of rectitude and benevolence. As Moseley says, the actions of the Commando prove that, when conditions are right, 'irony is a subtle weapon against totalitarianism' (156). In exposing the unflattering reality behind the slogans and political rhetoric of the powerful, the street theatre of the Commando has real substance; in this regard, it is the opposite of the empty, postmodernist spectacle of Petkanov's trial.

There is one other respect in which Barnes's novel is grounded in a way that is not typical of postmodernist fiction. His major characters do not in the end prove to be depthless, free-floating, wholly fragmented postmodern subjects, although Solinsky is at first presented so as to suggest that he is without psychological coherence and inner foundation. We are told that 'people [who] saw only Solinsky's outer life . . . tended to assume that his inner existence must be equally well ordered. In fact, he oscillated constantly between different levels of anxiety, and his intermittent thrusts of decisiveness were intended to allay the fret and stew within him' (36). Unlike Jean's father in *Staring at the Sun*, Solinsky's public roles as a member of society have not meshed seamlessly with his inner sense of who he is. Until he rebels by joining the Green Party, he tries with only partial success to mould his subjectivity from his family's and country's expectations of him as a Party member, a husband, and a father. When we first meet him in his role of Prosecutor in the trial of the former dictator, the narrator tells us that he is 'embarking on his most public form of self-definition' (37). He fails in this task of fashioning publicly an outward identity that can resolve his inner conflicts and solidify his sense of self, for, even though he wins a conviction, he feels in the end that he has been defeated and that Petkanov has triumphed. His marriage in ruins, his relationship with his daughter soured, Solinsky feels lost and dissatisfied.

Out of this very sense of defeat, paradoxically, comes Solinsky's brief recognition of an essential constituent of his selfhood. His final, private confrontation with Petkanov reads like a scene out of Dickens, Dostoevsky, or Conrad in which a dark *doppelgänger* claims identity with the protagonist. Seizing Solinsky's hand, Petkanov tells him,

> If I am a monster, I will come back to haunt your dreams, I will be your nightmare. If I am like you, I will come back to haunt your living days. . . . You cannot get rid of me. This farce of a trial makes no difference. Killing me would make no difference. . . . You can't get rid of me. Do you see? (136)

Solinksy not only sees but also feels this connection to the bottom of his being: 'He felt stained, contaminated, sexually corrupted, irradiated to the bone marrow' (136). Petkanov functions here, in what seems close to a psychoanalytic surface/depth model of identity, as a Jungian shadow, a fundamental archetype at the core of Solinsky's self that must be fully integrated into consciousness if he is to progress towards individuation. In this scene, there is a suggestion that Petkanov has mysteriously emerged from the impalpable realm of Solinsky's unconscious to assume an undeniably real solidity so that he can challenge Solinsky to accept a fundamental part of his own nature. In this regard, Pateman is perceptive in discerning that 'the initials of the two main characters are the same but in reverse— they are each other's alter ego and as such contain one another' (Pateman, *Julian Barnes* 64).

PART III
Criticism and Contexts

7

CRITICAL RECEPTION

Julian Barnes no longer reads reviews or criticism written about his books. He has said that

> I've never had a review which has told me something about the book that I didn't know already. I think that I am like most writers, I read criticism for its praise and I'm pleased by praise and displeased by blame, and this in a way is rather juvenile.... Criticism doesn't help you practically as a writer, so all you get is an emotional lifting-up or an emotional lowering-down. (Freiburg 48–9)

For any writer, even one as distinguished as Barnes, the experience of reading reviews is an emotional roller-coaster ride, because there are always some unflattering notices to counterbalance the positive ones. When Peter Aspden recently told him about the glowing reviews of the Mann-Booker Prize–nominated *Arthur & George*, Barnes replied, 'I am very glad you found some good ones, but I am sure you could find some bad ones too'. During the time when he did read reviews of his work, he noticed that 30 per cent were always positive, 30 per cent were negative, and 40 per cent were balanced, 'almost regardless of the book's quality' (Aspden 2). Having read scores of reviews of his books, I can attest that Barnes's view is accurate. In every case, including that of *Arthur & George*, there are some unflattering reviews to balance the positive ones, for the simple reason that no book meets the criteria for success of every reader. Even amongst the caste of professional reviewers and critics, tastes and expectations differ widely. Consequently, the body of criticism surveyed in this chapter is far from uniform in the opinions that it expresses about the worth of Barnes's writings. In some cases, the very qualities that are singled out for praise by one reviewer are damned by another.

Although *Metroland* was his first novel, some of its reviewers had expectations for it that were based on their familiarity with and respect for Barnes's work as a journalist. In the case of Paul Bailey, who found Barnes's columns on television 'consistently amusing and perceptive', the 'keen anticipation' with which he approached the novel was followed by disappointment (345). He found the coming-of-age narrative derivative and stale. In an altogether more favourable review, Nicholas Shrimpton declares that *Metroland* gratified his expectation that its prose would be elegantly crafted: 'No reader of the *New Statesman*, of course, needs to be told that Julian Barnes can put a good sentence together' (483). Tom Paulin also praises the style (63), and Sven Birkerts calls *Metroland* 'very much a *written* work, the product of a stylist with a strong pull toward Nabokovian artifice' ('Julian Barnes' 62).

As Matthew Pateman says (*Julian Barnes* 8), this literariness is not only a function of the style but also of the personality and preoccupations of the narrator-protagonist. Christopher Lloyd's comments on and allusions to cultural matters elicit a wide range of reactions from critics. Philip Sturgess concludes that the 'frequency of literary allusion and the general lack of any sense of a non-literary working world may depress those who feel they have encountered such ingredients rather too often in contemporary fiction' (10). Shrimpton notices 'a slight weakness for cultural name dropping', although he does express admiration for Barnes's treatment of adolescence (483). Bernard Levin identifies with Christopher's youthful aestheticism and exonerates Barnes of any charge of affectation or cultural snobbery (42). Like William Boyd (96), Levin extols Barnes's appreciation for and acceptance of the enthusiasms and foibles of youth (42). Both Frank Kermode, in his review of *Flaubert's Parrot* (15), and Edward Blishen, lend their voices to this choir of praise for *Metroland*'s treatment of the teenagers Chris and Toni. The first part of the novel, states Blishen, is 'a brilliantly funny account of overbright adolescence' (22). Writing after the novel's publication in the United States in 1987, Jay Parini also lauds Barnes's touching depiction 'of a friendship between two precociously erudite and witty adolescent boys', and he adds that this character type is 'almost inconceivable in American fiction' (1).

As Vanessa Guignery accurately notes (*Fiction* 12), however, not all of the views recorded about Barnes's powers of characterization are flattering. Bailey charges that '[t]here is a curious lack of people in *Metroland*, for all that their names are mentioned and some of their habits are described. . . . The single rounded character in the novel is Christopher's Uncle Arthur, a mean old sod who uses his nephew shamelessly' (345). Focusing on the female characters, Annick and Marion in particular, Levin, too, complains that Barnes 'has not yet fully mastered . . . the art of putting the blood as well as the bones in his characters' (42). Merritt Moseley defends Barnes by saying that the one-dimensionality of the subsidiary characters is a deliberate, appropriate feature in a novel that concentrates on the self-absorbed nature of adolescence: 'To the young Christopher, most people are fools or stooges or ridiculous bourgeois or possible targets of an "*epat*" or "*ecras*" ' (italics added) (21).

Nearly all of the reviewers and critics noticed the novel's symmetrical, tripartite structure. Shrimpton calls *Metroland* 'well constructed' (483), but Blishen finds it 'somehow too tidy, . . . too ably controlled, for the awkward thinking that's behind it' (22). Paulin, too, comments pejoratively on 'the sometimes arid effort at narrative geometry and pure style', but he also makes the contradictory remark that Barnes 'plays some extremely nimble tricks with the novel form' (63). Both Shrimpton and Parini admire the middle section that is set in Paris, Shrimpton calling it 'grippingly and sensitively done' (483) and Parini saying that '[o]ne would have to look hard to find a wryer, more lovingly detailed account of intellectual and sexual innocence abroad' (1–2). In contrast, David Williams criticizes the middle section on the grounds that it does not take advantage of its historical context and feature the exciting political events of 1968 (9). As Moseley (25) and Guignery (*Fiction* 10) say, though, Chris's obliviousness to the student protests is intrinsic to Barnes's thematic design, which is heavily ironic.

Frank Kermode lauds Barnes's second novel, *Before She Met Me*, as 'remarkably original and subtle' ('Obsessed' 15), and the most original aspect, the particular blending of genres that I discussed in Chapter 5, generated a good deal of critical commentary, both favourable and unfavourable. The mixture of comedy and lurid melodrama interested reviewers, although some, such as Anthony Thwaite, were disturbed by the violent subject matter:

> I am reluctant to bracket enjoyment as something to be gained from *Before She Met Me* except by readers of tough sensibilities. . . . Nimble verbal footwork, a succession of running gags and a tremendously winning assurance throughout don't, for me, quite compensate for the blind monomania one has to put up with in Graham's company. (31)

Gary Krist, too, seems troubled by the book's 'uneasy hybrid of comedy and melodrama' (1). But Kermode treats this same feature as one of the book's chief delights ('Obsessed' 15), as does Michiko Kakutani ('Books' C26). Moseley also expresses appreciation for Barnes's 'mixture of the comic and the macabre', and he notes that the book seems to combine 'the social observation, comedy, and verbal dexterity of *Metroland* with the queasy moral atmosphere and proximity to violence of *Duffy*' (54). Richard Todd, too, makes the connection between *Before She Met Me* and the Kavanagh novels, 'which might . . . be thought of as the product of a single imagination' (267).

As Guignery states (*Fiction* 17), several reviewers and critics saw parallels between *Before She Met Me*'s characters and those of *Metroland*. Bill Greenwell observes that 'Christopher [has been] revisited in Graham' and that, as a foil to the protagonist, the bohemian novelist Jack Lupton 'is an older Toni' (19). Richard Brown also affirms that Graham 'might be Chris Lloyd ten years on' (68), and David Leon Higdon makes this link as well (176). Pateman notices that in her straightforwardness and honesty Ann recalls Chris's love interests in *Metroland*: Annick and Marion (*Julian Barnes* 16).

Reviewers who were unfriendly to *Before She Met Me* tended to criticize its characters and their interactions on the grounds that they lack realism. Mark Abley states baldly that 'most of the characters are paper-thin. Graham's first wife is a caricature, their daughter a virtual cypher. Ann, the former actress who unwittingly provokes his obsession, seems strangely inert, and her behaviour is scarcely more believable than that of her husband' (456). Even Greenwell, in a largely positive review, has a reservation about the characterization of Ann (19), but Harriet Waugh finds her credible and admirable (17). Abley asserts that the plot is 'preposterous' (456), and John Mellors agrees that Barnes 'strain[s] our credulity until it snaps' ('Bull's Blood' 134). Krist finds the psychological transformation that Graham undergoes implausible (2), but Greenwell believes that Graham's 'breakdown is genuinely distressing, and subtly slow, so slow that we witness it with the same disbelief as Ann, as Jack, both helpless bystanders' (19). Moseley, in his study, argues that all of the major characters are fully rounded (65). Interestingly, none of the critics asks whether it is appropriate to hold a novel of ideas such as *Before She Met Me* to a standard of strict realism. Barnes himself has said that 'I don't think [that social realism is] where my talent lies. I can do bits of it, but it's part of a different construct' (Birnbaum, 'Robert Birnbaum' 6).

Most of the commentators on the novel deal in one way or another with its central subject of a civilized man's descent into savagery owing to the corrosive effect of obsessive jealousy. The grounding that the novel gives this breakdown in the neuropsychological theory of Paul Maclean sparked critical disagreement. Greenwell praises the way in which 'the battle between our rational and irrational selves' is 'woven playfully, effortlessly, and surreptitiously into the fabric of the novel' (19), whereas Birkerts attacks Barnes for relying 'too much on his theory and not enough upon the deeper psychology of disintegration' ('Julian Barnes' 63). Instead of focusing on the idea of warring parts of the brain, Mark Millington and Alison Sinclair relate Graham's predicament to the literary history of cuckoldry. They stress Barnes's originality in conflating two stereotypes in his treatment of Graham: the ridiculous cuckold, who is the passive dupe of an unfaithful wife, and the man of honour, who uses violence to punish those who have betrayed him (13–16).

Flaubert's Parrot was a truly magnificent achievement for Barnes, one that dramatically increased his standing in the literary community, and, owing to its formal ingenuity and intellectual richness, the book inspired not only reviews but also much academic criticism. One entire issue of the journal Q/W/E/R/T/Y, for example, was devoted to *Flaubert's Parrot*. As Moseley says, the generically mixed nature of the book 'inaugurated the ongoing controversy over whether the books Barnes writes are novels or something else—a controversy which, naturally enough, quieted down with his very different next novel, *Staring at the Sun*, but reignited with *A History of the World in 10¹/₂ Chapters*' (69). John Mellors says categorically that *Flaubert's Parrot* 'is not a novel at all. It is a collection of essays about Gustave Flaubert . . . written as if the essayist were not Barnes but a character invented by Barnes' ('Authorized Versions' 83). John Updike, too, concludes that *Flaubert's Parrot* neither looks like a novel nor delivers the narrative rewards of one: '[w]hile the novel as a form certainly asks for, and can absorb, a great deal of experimentation, it must at some point achieve self-forgetfulness and let pure event take over. In "Flaubert's Parrot," that point arrives too late, and brings too little' (87). Most critics were more flexibly inclined to celebrate the book as an unclassifiable literary work without worrying about whether it conforms to some predetermined definition of what a novel is. Peter Brooks, for example, calls *Flaubert's Parrot* 'a splendid hybrid of a novel, part biography, part fiction, part literary criticism, the whole carried off with great brio' (1). Barnes himself states that 'I can't think of *Flaubert's Parrot* as anything except a novel. I think if you withdrew the fictional infrastructure, it would just sort of collapse' (Freiburg 59). He would, I believe, approve of Michael Wood's astute remark that 'Barnes is not an essayist who writes novels, but a novelist who uses his imagination as an instrument of thought' (713).

Much of the criticism written on the novel focuses on Geoffrey Braithwaite, as both the protagonist and narrator. Updike, again, takes an antagonistic line in denying that the plight of the elderly widower is emotionally touching (87), and Melvyn Bragg agrees, saying that Geoffrey's 'tragedy—though planted as the deepest current in the book, did not draw me in' (23). Predictably, however, other reviewers advanced the opposed view. For instance, Kermode finds Geoffrey's account of his marriage, intertwined as it is with his researches into Flaubert, 'quite brilliantly written and deeply obsessive; the work of mourning is done by sifting through these surrogate and fading archives' ('Obsessed' 16)

Those who commented on Geoffrey's role as narrator were preoccupied with the self-consciousness and intrusiveness of his performance. Guignery is certainly right to emphasize the irony inherent 'in choosing an intrusive narrator in a book devoted to Flaubert, who specifically claimed the necessity for an impersonal type of narration' (*Fiction* 47). Higdon calls Geoffrey a 'reluctant' rather than unreliable narrator, because his diversions and interruptions are the result not of untrustworthiness but of having been traumatized by loss (174). But his self-consciousness as a narrator bespeaks not only his emotionally wounded condition but also his fraught epistemological and ontological context. As Alison Lee says, as a character he is a would-be realist, committed to the referential capacity of texts, but as a narrator he is a postmodernist who subverts those concerns (38–9). Both Neil Brooks (161) and Erica Hateley (*Flaubert's Parrot* 178) conceive of Geoffrey as a man trapped in a postmodernist world of plurality and indeterminacy who is nonetheless seeking an order and clarity that they identify as modernist.

Many reviewers noted that *Staring at the Sun* lacks the formal adventurousness and intellectual dazzle of *Flaubert' Parrot*, but Barnes's fourth novel nevertheless had many admirers as well as some detractors. Mark Lawson uncharitably remarks that 'after *Flaubert's Parrot* comes Barnes's Turkey'; he deplores the 'tired intricacy of its structure' and the characters' lack of substance ('Gender Bender' 53). David Lodge, who judges the book an 'honorable failure', charges that Gregory 'is a singularly colorless character, a mere mouthpiece for philosophical speculations that can't plausibly be attributed to his mother' ('Home Front' 21). Ian Hamilton also criticizes Gregory, whose emergence late in the novel as a major figure is evidence that 'the novelist has lost interest in the tale he first set out to tell', and Hamilton also complains that the perpetually bemused Jean 'is portrayed as near-retarded, according to any conventional definition of brain power' (7). But for Mira Stout, *Staring at the Sun* is '[a]rguably Barnes's strongest novel', one that 'balances grand themes with gemlike wit' (5). And the Mexican novelist Carlos Fuentes refers to it as 'brilliant' (1); he praises it and Barnes's other novels for being 'at the forefront of a new internationalization of British fiction' (4).

Many of the critics concentrated on the topics that I discussed in the previous chapter: the ordinariness of the novel's protagonist, the feminist implications of her quest for freedom, the novel's tripartite structure, its generic heterogeneity, the development of the story through 'leitmotifs rather than a densely woven narrative' (Lodge 'Home Front' 21), and themes such as the nature of courage and the quest for meaning in a boundless, enigmatic universe. Fuentes observes that the 'novel flashes between the extremes of enchantment and disenchantment' and argues that 'Jean belongs to both the magical and the utilitarian worlds' (1). In a similar vein, Alison Hennegan (38), Ann Hulbert (38), and Moseley (101) say that the novel explores the paradoxically extraordinary dimensions of mundane existence. Lodge ('Home Front' 21) and Pateman (*Julian Barnes* 37–8) discuss the feminist aspects of Jean's story and her relationship with Gregory's girlfriend, Rachel. Pateman analyses the different generic conventions activated in each of the novel's three sections (*Julian Barnes* 35–40), and Guignery examines each of them in relation to the epigraphs that precede them (*Fiction* 56–8). Fuentes (2), Hulbert (38), Hennegan (39), Pateman (*Julian Barnes* 34), Moseley (105), and Guignery (*Fiction* 51–3) investigate the thematic implications of the novel's metaphors and symbols, such as the sun and the airplanes.

Frank Kermode, in his review of A *History of the World in 10¹/₂ Chapters*, was prophetic in saying that 'this book might well provide texts for academic discussions about history and fable' ('Stowaway' 20). Like *Flaubert's Parrot*, A *History* did over time spawn numerous academic articles on that very topic, in addition to the inevitable reviews that appeared shortly after the book was published. Many of the commentators insisted on the brilliance of Barnes's accomplishment in this most unorthodox of novels. Brown states that Barnes 'confronts history with postmodern theories of representation to produce the most successful yet of his novels' (68), and Anthony Quinn concurs: 'A *History of the World in 10¹/₂ Chapters* shapes up not only as Barnes's funniest novel but also [as] his most richly cargoed and imaginatively designed' (38). Kermode, however, confesses to feeling 'cool' about A *History*, charging that the author's need to be wry 'produces moments when that self-deprecating flipness spoils the tone' ('Stowaway' 20). Robert Adams also bridles against the 'sardonic' tone of the individual chapters 'written...at a temperature not far from zero centigrade' (7). The American novelist Joyce Carol Oates, though, seems not only to admire the book's tone but also to disagree about its qualities; for her it is characterized by 'gentle, humane, self-reflective irony' (3). Another complaint about *A History*, made by Kermode, pertains to its alleged lack of coherence; he charges that the linkages amongst the chapters are too weak ('Stowaway' 20). Birkerts also doubts whether the novel's form as a postmodernist collage lends it enough unity of purpose: '*A History of the World in 10½ Chapters* is finally a book without a significant point' ('Julian Barnes' 66), he claims.

These criticisms about the text's lack of wholeness stem from the more basic perception that it does not really deserve the label 'novel' to which it lays claim. Robert Adams says sarcastically that the book is 'about as much entitled to the name of a "novel" as to the name *A History of the World*' (7). Oates, too, says that 'Julian Barnes's fifth book is neither the novel it is presented as being nor the breezy pop history of the world its title suggests'; it is, she says, 'most usefully described as a gathering of prose pieces, some fiction, others rather like essays' (1). D. J. Taylor joins the chorus when he says that '*A History of the World in 10½ Chapters* is not a novel, according to the staider definitions; it possesses no character who rises above the level of a cipher and no plot worth speaking of'. He concludes, however, that the book is, after all, 'a significant novel' because it possesses the *sine qua non* of the genre in its contemporary manifestation: a postmodernist self-consciousness ('Newfangled' 40). Barnes's justification for calling the text a novel is that 'it was conceived as a whole and executed as a whole. Things in it thicken and deepen. . . . I suppose what it boils down to is that if you don't like it, it's a collection of short stories. If you do, it's a novel' (quoted in Cook 10).

In their reviews of *Talking It Over*, more than one critic commented on the limited scope of the novel in comparison with the very ambitious *A History of the World in 10½ Chapters*, and for some the small-scale, domestic character of the novel's subject matter, a romantic triangle, rendered it insignificant. Mick Imlah states that 'Julian Barnes has chosen a small canvas, three lightweight characters and a boring title'. He concludes that the book is 'skil-fully executed but scarcely memorable' (19). Charles Nicholl judges *Talking It Over* 'a minor work in the Barnes canon: enjoyable but not very challenging' (19). Imlah complains that the work's struc-ture is too schematic, in that the action of the second half too neatly reflects that of the first (19), and D. J. Taylor concurs, say-ing that it 'is a novel of deliberate and occasionally rather stifling symmetry' ('Fearful Symmetry' 4). Taylor's objections to Barnes's novel encompass what he takes to be the banality of one of its main themes: 'that frightful chestnut, the subjective nature of truth' ('Fearful Symmetry' 4). Josephine Humphreys, though, who draws attention to the same theme, praises the novel's 'interplay of seri-ous thought and dazzling wit'. 'This story is more than credible', she says; 'it's moving, it's funny, it's frightening' (1). For Philip Howard, the novel's narrow focus on three individuals does not reduce its importance, since it also offers insights into the culture at large: 'It is, of course, quick-silver clever and allusive, funny about things nobody else bothers to write about. . . . Its cultural credentials are brilliant' (16).

The topics that interested most of the commentators on *Talking It Over* were the unusual narrative technique employed by Barnes, the distinctive qualities of the voices of the three protagonists, and the principal themes: love, jealousy, betrayal, and the sub-jective nature of truth. As Moseley notes, the narrative method 'raises interesting philosophical questions . . . about the ontology of fictional creations. It is self-conscious fiction' (139). As fictional characters, Gillian, Stuart, and Oliver are entirely constituted by the words of their speeches. The flamboyant and highly articulate Oliver's self-fashioning through language was singled out by crit-ics; as Imlah remarks, he is 'all expression' (19). Moseley observes that in exposing the volatility of love over the course of the novel Barnes also reveals 'the evanescence or inaccessibility of truth' (125). Pateman adds that *Talking It Over* 'foreground[s] the problems of judgement and veracity, with particular emphasis in the story on their relationship to love and truth' (*Julian Barnes* 55).

Many of the reviewers of Barnes's next novel, *The Porcupine*, tried to gauge his degree of success in writing as a foreigner about the politics of Bulgaria. Barnes, after all, does not speak the language, and he is relatively unfamiliar with the nation's culture and history.

Michael Scammell contrasts him invidiously to other English-speaking writers, such as Malcolm Bradbury and Saul Bellow, who focalized 'their narratives through Western eyes': '[t]he attempt to narrate events from the inside marks an uncharacteristic tactical error on Barnes's part' (4). According to John Bayley, the consequences of his failed imaginative leap are characters that lack credibility: 'they become lay figures, as stiff and symbolic as the bronze statues of Lenin and Stalin and the Heroic Russian Soldier now being carted away to a scrapheap behind the railway station' (32). The political dialogue that they engage in has, for him, a 'leaden obviousness' (31). Scammell also criticizes the characters, branding them as 'the stock figures of socialist realism': 'the feisty, can-do commissar', 'the wimpy intellectual', and 'the wise old woman' (4). Robert Stone, too, is disappointed by the 'obviousness' of the world created in the book, which is 'so short that its characters have only enough time to represent the political attitudes assigned to them. It is possible, at the outset, to know what everyone will have to say' (3).

For some critics, however, such as Robert Harris, the novel's 'East European background is expertly rendered', its characters come vividly to life, and its political issues are treated profoundly. Petkanov, the deposed Communist dictator, is 'a satirical creation of genius', and the novel, taken as a whole, 'is a minor masterpiece of political satire: compelling, funny, and frightening' (26). Richard Eder also praises the creation of Petkanov, 'a joyfully rich character' ('History' 3). Whereas Bayley criticizes the exchanges between Petkanov and Solinsky as inert, Patrick Parrinder praises those same passages, calling them 'crackling Shavian dialogues between the Prosecutor and the ex-President' (18). Unlike Scammell, James Atlas does not conclude that the schematic nature of the novel's characterization is a flaw (although he does believe that the characters could be better developed), for he sees that the book 'has the allegorical feel of a novel by Kundera (another French novelist who happens not to be French)' (188). It might be more appropriate, in other words, to assess *The Porcupine* as a novel of ideas rather than to condemn it out of hand as lacking in social realism. For Maureen Howard, unlike for Stone, the novel's brevity (it is 'more a pamphlet or broadside than a novella') is not a weakness, since '*The Porcupine* is a delightful book in which [Barnes] accomplishes what he sets out to do in a very short time' (134).

Most of the critics who wrote on the novel that followed *The Porcupine* in 1998, the highly acclaimed *England, England*, commented on the implications of the fantasy at its heart: the shrunken, superficial replica of England that Sir Jack Pitman builds on the Isle of Wight as a tourist destination. Many of the reviewers judged the central conceit to be, as Richard Eder puts it, 'smart and accomplished' (2), and some, such as David Wiegand, noted the respects in which it reflects and satirizes an actual blight afflicting Britain's culture: '*England, England* [is] a wonderfully nasty satire on Britannia's drifting sense of history and identity' (1). Several critics, such as Randall Curb (1), also explained how Barnes's concern in the novel with the 'invention of tradition' dovetails with the obsessive interest that he has shown in other books in the human tendency to fabricate the past. For Ian Sansom, despite their diversity, all of Barnes's books, including *England, England*, 'seem eventually to revolve and resolve around the simple toothcracking question of the relationship between truth and fiction' (31). Guignery adds 'the elusive nature of memory' to the list of themes that the novel shares with Barnes's other works of fiction (*Fiction* 105).

James Miracky analyses the uses to which Barnes puts Jean Baudrillard's theories about postmodernist culture, arguing that *England, England* both draws on and overturns those theories:

> Barnes satirizes both the world of hyperreality and that of critical theory, in effect creating a parody of a parody, or a novel that continually turns in on itself. Just when one suspects that Barnes is validating postmodern theory, he incorporates elements that reach for an authentic human experience of the real, ultimately leaving the novel positioned somewhere between homage and parody of the dominance of the 'hyperreal'. (2)

Both Stevenson (48) and Head also believe that elements of the novel suggest a humanistic affiliation that counteracts the tendency of postmodernist simulacra to decentre human experience. In Head's words, there is 'a dynamic in the book that is at variance with this insistence on the false or artificial elements of history and identity' (120). Most of the critical discussions of this quest for the real revolve around Martha Cochrane's love affair with Paul

Harrison and the pastoral elements of the presentation of Anglia in the novel's third part.

The majority of the critics who wrote on Barnes's next novel, *Love, etc.*, concentrated on topics that I discussed earlier in this chapter, in relation to *Talking It Over*: the unusual narrative technique, the opportunities for readerly involvement that it affords, and the themes that emerge naturally from it, such as the relativity of truth. Not surprisingly, the reviewers also focused on the relationship of *Love, etc.* to the earlier novel. Since *Love, etc.* is a sequel that takes up the story of Gillian, Stuart, and Oliver some ten years after the point at which *Talking It Over* concluded, Barnes's readers were interested in the way that the narrative of the love triangle develops and radically reverses its course. Several reviewers, such as Erin McGraw, remarked on how in *Love, etc.* 'the frolicsome spirit of the first book gives way to a darker vision, closer to despair' (1). Elaine Showalter, who characterizes the novel as 'the gothic version of *Talking It Over*, in which romantic comedy has turned into madness and horror' (3), considers it less successful than its predecessor because the transformation of the characters does not seem to her psychologically believable: 'They seem to be acting out a schematic reversal of fortune, rather than deepening our understanding' (4). Michiko Kakutani, too, calls *Love, etc.* 'a book that suffers from phoniness and authorial manipulation, a novel that for all its easy readability lacks its predecessor's persuasiveness and charm' ('Love, Etc.' 1).

Susannah Herbert, however, holds that *Love, etc.* is 'even better than the earlier book' (4), and McGraw enumerates one important respect in which *Love, etc.* offers a deeper insight into life's sometimes destabilizing revelations than does *Talking It Over*: '[m]ore insistently than its predecessor, *Love, etc.* is concerned with how we perceive our own lives, and how easily a shift in perceptions can defamiliarize the most familiar assumptions, making a spouse seem a stranger' (2). McGraw is referring here to particular examples in the novel of the ways in which 'old actions assume new patterns. What had once appeared to be Gillian's great gesture of love from *Talking It Over* comes to look like self-serving deception. Stuart's chivalric devotion is revealed to be coarse, even base' (2). Pateman lauds another, related, aspect of *Love, etc.*: the power with which it treats 'the loss of faith and the lack of myth in the contemporary world' (*Julian Barnes* 84), a topic that preoccupies Barnes in all of his work. Pateman notes with acuity that the 'bleakness of *Love, etc.* derives not only from each of the characters' own personal torments, but also because these torments are linked by the characters to broader concerns regarding the loss of faith, the lack of any structures within which to place themselves, the collapse of the sustaining metaphysical categories' (*Julian Barnes* 85).

One other facet of the novel that drew some critical attention is its open ending and the controversy over whether or not Stuart does indeed rape Gillian. For Sven Birkerts, the conclusion is anti-climactic:

> Barnes must find a way to discharge the tensions he has created. Alas, he elects late in the book to make everything turn on a half-drunk, fumbling assault on Gillian by Stuart. Though in equal parts touching and humiliating, the scene isn't big enough or resonant enough to resolve the deeper issue that Barnes has begun to point to: the whole mucky business of repossessing love in the wake of mutual betrayals. ('Talking' 4)

What Birkerts does not take into account is that in a novel as open to life's confusions and ambiguities as *Love, etc.*, a neat resolution of the issues and dilemmas at stake might not be what is called for. And the tawdry sexual assault (if such it was) might well be a perfectly appropriate action for the conclusion of a novel so directly concerned with the waning of idealism and the embitterment of the characters as they age. Of course, the open ending also paves the way for Barnes to create yet another sequel. 'I hope he writes it', opines Birkerts,

> [n]ot just because I so enjoy the rumble and swerve of his prose but because he needs to recover and dramatize some of that sense of *amour fou* that drove the first novel and began to expire here. Love—tragic or ecstatic—must be allowed to carry the day over mere etc. ('Talking' 3)

Arthur & George, Barnes's most recent novel, struck many reviewers as being refreshingly different from the other works in his canon. Natasha Walter contrasts this 'leisurely historical novel' with the 'sharp brisk fiction' that he had published previously. Whereas *Flaubert's Parrot*, his earliest excursion into the historical past, was a 'quirky, challenging novel', *Arthur & George* 'delivers the conventional pleasures of historical fiction; of watching the past recreated with painstaking detail' (26). In a similar vein, Theo Tait calls the book 'a sustained, uninterrupted exercise in quasi-documentary fiction, prefigured only by Barnes's most untypical work, *The Porcupine* (1992)' (26). Several critics observed that in *Arthur & George* Barnes not only sets his tale in the early twentieth century but also attempts a stylistic pastiche of Edwardian fiction. One of them, Simon O'Hagan, lauds the 'elegance and restraint of Barnes's narrative voice, echoing as it does the formality of prose of the period' (1). Tait and Robert Hanks (2) praise Barnes for accepting the past on its own terms rather than trying to refashion it in the image of the present. As Tait notes, though, his lack of condescension to his forbears does not prevent the development of a certain amount of irony: '[h]e re-creates the period sympathetically, and does not patronize its attitudes, but has an excellent eye for its straight-faced and sometimes rather malevolent absurdities' (26). Notwithstanding his refusal to treat the past anachronistically, Barnes has said that the issues with which he contends in the text seem 'to be completely relevant to today' (Robinson 2). As I pointed out in my Introduction, the novel's preoccupation with racial scapegoating and social unease is a highly contemporary concern.

If *Arthur & George* signals an exciting new departure for Barnes, there are also important respects in which it reworks some of the methods and themes of his earlier books. Guignery notes one respect in which *Arthur & George* resembles, rather than differs from, many of the author's other works of fiction: it 'mixes reality and imagination so that the book is part history, part biography and part fiction' (*Fiction* 129). Andrew Crumey also comments on the novel's blend of historical information with invented details, praising 'the seamless way in which [the] facts are woven into a compelling narrative' (1). Lewis Jones discerns that *Arthur & George* resembles *Flaubert's Parrot* in being 'an exercise in literary and historical detection' (1). Stuart Jeffries suggests that *Arthur & George* revisits *England, England*, in the sense that both texts explore the nature of Englishness, and Barnes himself endorses this reading (2–3). Guignery draws attention to the parallel beginnings of *Arthur & George*; *England, England*; *Talking It Over*; and *Love, etc.*; she notices that all of these novels interrogate the reliability of memory by starting 'with the issue of what one remembers' (*Fiction* 128). Also focusing on the issue of memory in *Arthur & George*, Jon Barnes links what he calls its 'tricksiness' to the 'phenomenon of historical slippage'. He shrewdly perceives that *Arthur & George* 'marks a return to one of the most resonant themes of Barnes's *oeuvre*, the malleability of the past, the untrustworthiness of history'. The defamiliarizing effect of this scepticism about the veracity of historical narratives has, for Jon Barnes, the paradoxical effect of making Julian Barnes's own representations of history in *Arthur & George* seem 'palpable, surprising, and real' (19).

I agree with the many critics who celebrated *Arthur & George* as a splendid artistic accomplishment. Kemp, for example, concludes his review by saying that 'Barnes's suave, elegant prose—alive here with precision, irony, and humaneness—has never been used better than in this extraordinary true-life tale' (38), and the distinguished crime novelist P. D. James says that

> [f]rom the first paragraphs we know ourselves to be in the hands of a major novelist and are borne forward by a compelling narrative, beautifully controlled, which combines the satisfactions of biography, social history and the excitement and ratiocination of a real-life detective story. This novel is Barnes at his best. (7)

As Guignery says, *Arthur & George* is yet more evidence of Barnes's determination to make each new work of fiction fresh and original. 'The diversity of his literary production to date', she says, 'clearly demonstrates that the author never stops experimenting with form, style and subject matter' (*Fiction* 132). The only prediction that can be ventured about his future publications is that they too will surprise and delight his many readers.

NOTES

3 *METROLAND* AND *ARTHUR & GEORGE*

1. In answer to questions about the possible influence of critical theory on his work, Barnes has stated that he has read very little of it, but he allows that ideas derived from theory that have entered the zeitgeist might well have affected his thinking (Freiburg 52–3).
2. In the very titles that he has chosen for the four parts of *Arthur & George*, Barnes has emphasized the crucial role played by beginnings and endings in determining the meanings of narratives: Beginnings, Beginning with an Ending, Ending with a Beginning, and Endings.
3. Arthur shares this obsession with his creator. Barnes has said that from the age of 16 not a day has gone by during which he has not thought about death (O'Regan 1).

4 *FLAUBERT'S PARROT, A HISTORY OF THE WORLD IN 10½ CHAPTERS,* AND *ENGLAND, ENGLAND*

1. Andrzej Gasiorek provides a succinct summary of the ideas promulgated by recent theorists of history that challenge traditional views (147–9). As he states, opposition 'to the positivists' scientific elaboration of a covering law model has come from a variety of sources— feminist, Marxist, narrativist, post-structuralist, post-colonial, New Historicist. These different theoretical perspectives all question history's claims to know the past' (147).
2. For two examples, see Gasiorek (158–65) and Childs (89–99).
3. Christopher Tayler remarks that all through his career as a novelist Barnes has shown an imaginative empathy with the lives of elderly people (17). It is tempting to ask whether the 21-year-old Chris in *Metroland* is speaking for his creator when he tells Marion that 'I long to be a sprightly sixty-five. . . . It's as if everyone has a perfect age to which they aspire, and they're only truly at ease with themselves when they get there' (114).
4. I have written previously on Swift's novel. See 'The Representation of History as Plastic: The Search for the Real Thing in Graham Swift's *Ever After'. Ariel* 27.3 (1996): 25–43.

5. The French thinker hired by Sir Jack to give the Project an intellectual cachet alludes to Guy Debord's *The Society of the Spectacle*, which lamented the reduction of lived experience to 'mere representation' (*England, England* 56).
6. Barnes told Guignery that he had never heard of, much less read, Williams-Ellis's book before he wrote *England, England* (*Fiction* 106, 148).

5 *BEFORE SHE MET ME, TALKING IT OVER,* AND *LOVE, ETC.*

1. The *fabula*, according to Seymour Chatman, is 'the basic story stuff, the sum total of events', whereas the *szujet* is 'the story as actually told by linking the events together' (19–20). Since Barnes's *fabula* spans ten years, he necessarily omits many of its probable events from the *sjuzets* of the two novels.
2. This comparison between the characters' intimate, direct communications with us and personal letters perhaps helps to explain why Barnes wrote a sequel to *Talking It Over* and why he has said that he is contemplating writing another volume to round out the trilogy (Birnbaum, 'Interview' 10). A correspondence between two people, one of A. S. Byatt's characters in *Possession* observes, is 'a form of narrative that envisages no outcome, no closure' (130–1). The sense of ongoingness inherent in the form perhaps helped to spark the realization that Barnes had after writing *Talking It Over* that 'there was still a lot to happen in the lives of the characters' (Brotton 1).
3. According to Erica Hateley, *Talking It Over* illustrates that within patriarchy economic relations between males govern the dynamics of the erotic triangle. She holds that Gillian's 'voice is always responsive, often passive and rarely independent' ('Erotic Triangles' 6). Hateley's analysis is insightful, but she overlooks the considerable degree to which Gillian exerts control over Stuart and Oliver. As Guignery rightly says, the 'distribution of power in this triangular relationship turns out to be much more complex than it appears at first reading' (*Fiction* 82).

6 *STARING AT THE SUN* AND *THE PORCUPINE*

1. When Leslie first proposes that Jean play the shoelace game with him, readers might suspect that this is a euphemism for imminent sexual abuse, but the connection between the game and sex proves to be more indirect than this.

2. Barnes stated in an interview that he expected critics to apply the adjective 'Orwellian' to the novel (Banner 10), and I am happy to oblige.
3. There are critics who do analyse the novel as a political satire. See Agudo and Lázaro.
4. This point was first made by Sesto (123).

BIBLIOGRAPHY

Abley, Mark. 'Watching Green-Eyed.' Rev. of *Before She Met Me*. *Times Literary Supplement* 23 April 1982: 456.

Adams, Robert. 'Balancing Act.' Rev. of *A History of the World in 10¹/₂ Chapters*. *The New York Review of Books* 26 October 1989: 7.

Adams, Tim. 'Show Me the Way to Go, Holmes.' Rev. of *Arthur & George*. *Guardian Weekly* 8–14 July 2005: 25.

——. 'The Eternal Triangle.' Rev. of *Love, etc*. *Observer* 23 July 2000. http://books.guardian.co.uk/print/0,3858,4043244-99930,00.html/4/24/2006.

Agudo, Juan Francisco Elices. 'What is Right and What is Wrong in Politics? Objects of Satire in Julian Barnes.' *The Porcupine*.' *Revista Canaria de Estudios Ingleses* 39 (1999): 295–305.

Amis, Martin. *Experience*. Toronto: Knopf Canada, 2000.

——. 'Interview.' Interview Conducted by Eleanor Wachtel. *The Malahat Review* 114 (1996): 43–58.

Arnold, Matthew. *Poetry and Criticism of Matthew Arnold*. Ed. A. Dwight Culler. Boston: Riverside-Houghton Mifflin, 1961.

——. 'To a Friend.' In *Poetical Works*. Ed. C. B. Tinker and H. S. Lowry. London: Oxford UP, 1950. 2.

Aspden, Peter. 'Loyal Supporter Novelist Julian Barnes Could Not Bring Himself to Join the Frenzy of Commentators after the London Bombings—He Felt More Comfortable Talking about the Olympics and Leicester City.' *The Financial Times* 16 July 2005: 1–3.

Atlas, James. 'Courtroom Drama.' Rev. of *The Porcupine*. *Vogue* November 1992: 188, 190.

Auden, W. H. 'Who's Who.' In *Collected Poems*. Ed. Edward Mendelson. New York: Random House, 1976. 109.

Bakhtin, Mikhail. *Problems of Dostoevsky's Poetics*. Theory and History of Literature Series. Volume 8. Ed. and Trans. Caryl Emerson. Minneapolis: University of Minnesota Press, 1984.

——. *Rabelais and His World*. 1965. Trans. Helene Iswolsky. Bloomington: Midland-Indiana UP, 1984.

——. *The Dialogic Imagination: Four Essays*. Trans. Caryl Emerson and Michael Holquist. Austin: University of Texas Press, 1981.

Bailey, Paul. 'Settling for Suburbia.' Rev. of *Metroland*. *TLS* 28 March 1980: 345.

Baldick, Chris. *The Concise Oxford Dictionary of Literary Terms*. Oxford: Oxford UP, 1990.

Banner, Simon. 'Word Painter's Brush with the Future.' *The Times* [London] 20 September 1986: 10.

Barnes, Jon. 'The Pig-Chaser's Tale.' Rev. of *Arthur & George*. *TLS* 8 July 2005: 19.

Barnes, Julian. *A History of the World in 10¹/₂ Chapters*. New York: Knopf, 1989.

———. *Arthur & George*. London: Jonathan Cape, 2005.

———. *Before She Met Me*. 1982. London: Picador-Pan, 1983.

———. 'Candles for the Living.' *London Review of Books* 22 November 1990: 6–7.

———. *Cross Channel*. New York: Knopf, 1996.

———. *Duffy* (under pseudonym Dan Kavanagh). London: Jonathan Cape, 1980.

———. *England, England*. New York: Vintage-Random House, 1998.

———. *Fiddle City* (under pseudonym Dan Kavanagh). 1981. London: Penguin, 1988.

———. *Flaubert's Parrot* (1984). London: Picador-Pan, 1985.

———. *Going to the Dogs* (under pseudonym Dan Kavanagh). New York: Pantheon-Random House, 1987.

———. *Letters from London*. Toronto: Vintage Canada-Random House, 1995.

———. *Love, etc*. Toronto: Vintage Canada-Random House, 2000.

———. *Metroland*. 1980. New York: McGraw-Hill, 1987.

———. *Putting the Boot In* (under pseudonym Dan Kavanagh). London: Jonathan Cape, 1985.

———. *Something to Declare*. London: Picador-Pan Macmillan, 2002.

———. *Staring at the Sun*. 1986. Toronto: Random House, 1987.

———. 'Stranger than Fiction.' *New Yorker* 26 October 1992: 140.

———. *Talking It Over*. Toronto: Vintage International-Random House, 1991.

———. 'The Follies of Writer Worship.' In *The Best American Essays 1986*. Ed. Elizabeth Hardwick. New York: Ticknor & Fields, 1986. 1–8.

———. *The Lemon Table*. New York: Random House, 2004.

———. 'The Past Conditional.' *New Yorker* 35 December 2006 and 1 January 2007: 56–64.

———. *The Pedant in the Kitchen*. London: Atlantic, 2003.

———. *The Porcupine*. New York: Knopf, 1992.

Bayley, John. 'Time of Indifference.' Rev. of *The Porcupine*. *New York Review of Books* 17 December 1992: 30–2.

Begley, Adam. 'What Lies Beneath.' *Details* 19.5 (2001): 86–8.

Belsey, Catherine. *Critical Practice*. New Accents. London: Routledge, 1980.

Benjamin, Walter. 'Theses on the Philosophy of History.' In *Illuminations*. 1970. Trans. Harry Zohn. London: Fontana-Harper Collins, 1992, 245–55.

Bennett, Andrew and Nicholas Royle. *An Introduction to Literature, Criticism, and Theory: Key Critical Concepts*. Hemel Hempstead: Prentice Hall/Harvester Wheatsheaf, 1995.

Billen, Andrew. 'Two Aspects of a Writer.' *Observer* 7 July 1991: 26.

Birkerts, Sven. 'Julian Barnes (1946–).' In *British Writers*. Ed. by George Stade and Carol Howard. New York: Scribners, 1997, pp. 65–76. Rpt. in *Contemporary Literary Criticism*. Volume 141. Ed. Justin Karr. Farmington Hills, MI: Gale, 2001. 61–70.

———. 'Talking It Over Some More.' Rev. of *Love, etc. New York Times* 9 February 2001.   http://www.nytimes.com/books/01/02/25/reviews/010225.25birkert.html.

Birnbaum, Robert. 'Interview: Julian Barnes, Etc.' http://www.identity-theory.com/people/birnbaum8.html/1/21/2005.

———. 'Robert Birnbaum Interviews Julian Barnes.' 1999. http://www.julianbarnes.com/resources/birnbaum-ee.html/5/13/2007.

Blishen, Edward. 'Growing up.' Rev. of *Metroland*. *Times Educational Supplement* 2 May 1980: 22.

Boccardi, Mariadele. 'Biography, the Postmodern Last Frontier: Banville, Barnes, Byatt, and Unsworth.' *Q/W/E/R/T/Y* 11 (2001): 149–57.

Boyd, William. 'Late Sex.' Rev. of *Metroland*. *London Magazine* October 1980: 95–6.

Bradbury, Malcolm. *The Modern British Novel*. 1993. London: Penguin, 1994.

Bragg, Melvyn. 'In Fine Feather.' Rev. of *Flaubert's Parrot*. *Punch* 17 October 1984: 22–3.

Brooks, Neil. 'Silence of the Parrots: Repetition and Interpretation in *Flaubert's Parrot*.' *Q/W/E/R/T/Y* 11 (2001): 159–66.

Brooks, Peter. 'Obsessed with the Hermit of Croisset.' Rev. of *Flaubert's Parrot*. *New York Times Book Review* 10 March 1985. http://www.nytimes.com/books/01/02/25/specials/barnes-parrot.html.

Brotton, Jerry. 'Let's Talk about Love, etc.: An Interview with Julian Barnes.' http://www.amazon.co.uk/exec/obidos/tg/feature/-/66610/ref=pd_d_ra_rab_1_1/qid=96959 . . . /1/22/2005.

Brown, Richard (Updated by Tobias Wachinger). 'Barnes, Julian (Patrick).' In *Contemporary Novelists*, 7th Edition. Ed. Neil Schlager and Josh Lauer. Detroit: St. James-Gale Group, 2001. 67–9.

Buchan, James. 'An Unsuccessful Likeness.' Rev. of *Talking It Over*. *Spectator* 20 July 1991: 25–6.

Buxton, Jackie. 'Julian Barnes's Theses on History (in 10½ Chapters).' *Contemporary Literature* 41.1 (2000): 56–86.

Chatman, Seymour. *Story and Discourse: Narrative Structure in Fiction and Film.* Ithaca: Cornell UP, 1978.

Childs, Peter. *Contemporary Novelists: British Fiction since 1970.* Basingstoke: Palgrave Macmillan, 2005.

Clark, Katrina and Michael Holquist. *Mikhail Bakhtin.* Cambridge: Belknapp-Harvard UP, 1984.

Collingwood, R. G. *The Idea of History.* Rev. ed. 1983. Ed. Jan Van Der Dussen. Oxford: Oxford UP, 1994.

Cook, Bruce. 'The World's History and then Some in 10½ Chapters.' *Los Angeles Daily News* 7 November 1989: L10.

Crumey, Andrew. 'Stranger than any Fiction.' Rev. of *Arthur & George. Scotland on Sunday* 3 July 2005. http://news.scotsman.com/print.cfm?id= 739242005/9/3/2005.

Culler, Jonathan. *Framing the Sign: Criticism and Its Institutions.* Norman: University of Oklahoma Press, 1988.

Curb, Randall. Rev. of *England, England.* Fiction Book Page http://www. bookpage.com/9905bp/fiction/england_england.html/11/9/2005.

Dening, Penelope. 'Inventing England.' *The Irish Times* 8 September 1998. http://web.lexisnexis.com/universe/printdoc/11/21/2005.

Duplain, Julian. 'The Big Match.' Rev. of *The Porcupine. New Statesman and Society* 13 November 1992: 34–5.

Eder, Richard. 'History, Take Two.' Rev. of *The Porcupine. Los Angeles Times* 8 November 1992: 3.

——. 'Tomorrowland.' Rev. of *England, England. New York Times* 9 May 1999. http://www.nytimes.com/books/99/05/09/reviews/990509.09ederlt. html/ 1/22/2005.

Elias, Justine. 'Metroland.' *Village Voice* 6 April 1999. http://www.village-voice. com/film/9914,elias2,4831,20.html/4/7/2008.

Finney, Brian. 'A Worm's Eye View of History: Julian Barnes's *A History of the World in 10½ Chapters.*' 28 January 2005. http://www.csulb.edu/~bhfinney/Barnes.html.

Freiburg, Rudolf. 'Julian Barnes.' In *Do You Consider Yourself a Postmodern Author? Interviews with Contemporary English Writers.* Ed. Rudolf Freiburg and Jan Schnitker. Munster: Lit Verlag, 1999. 41–66.

Fuentes, Carlos. 'The Enchanting Blue Yonder.' Rev. of *Staring at the Sun. New York Times* 12 April 1987. http://www.nytimes.com/books/01/02/25/specials/barnes-staring.html/1/22/2005.

Gasiorek, Andrzej. *Post-War British Fiction: Realism and After.* London: Edward Arnold, 1995.

Graves, Robert. 'My Name and I.' *Robert Graves: Poems Selected by Himself.* 4th Edition. Harmondsworth: Penguin, 1972. 106–7.

Greenwell, Bill. 'Flashback.' Rev. of *Before She Met Me. New Statesman* 16 April 1982: 18–19.

Guignery, Vanessa. '"History in Question(s)": An Interview with Julian Barnes.' *Sources* 8 (2000): 59–72.

——. 'Julian Barnes in Conversation.' *Cercles* 4 (2002): 255–69. http://www.cercles.com/n4/barnes.pdf.

——. *The Fiction of Julian Barnes: A Reader's Guide to Essential Criticism.* Basingstoke: Palgrave MacMillan, 2006.

Hall, Donald E. *Subjectivity.* The New Critical Idiom. New York: Routledge, 2004.

Hamilton, Ian. 'Real Questions.' Rev. of *Staring at the Sun. London Review of Books* 6 November 1986: 7.

Hanks, Robert. 'Julian Barnes: Resurrecting Sir Arthur Conan Doyle.' *Independent* 2 September 2005. http://enjoyment.independent.co.uk/books/interviews/articles297 543.ece/9/2/2005.

Hardy, Thomas. 'He Never Expected Much.' In *Thomas Hardy.* Ed. Samuel Hynes. Oxford: Oxford UP, 1984. 452.

Harris, Robert. 'Full of Prickles.' Rev. of *The Porcupine. Literary Review* November 1992: 26.

Hateley, Erica. 'Erotic Triangles in Amis and Barnes: Negotiations of Patriarchal Power.' *Lateral* 3 (2001). http://www.julianbarnes.com/sr/eroti-triangles.html/1/28/2005.

——. '*Flaubert's Parrot* as Modernist Quest.' *Q/W/E/R/T/Y* 11 (2001): 177–81.

Head, Dominic. *The Cambridge Introduction to Modern British Fiction, 1950–2000.* Cambridge: Cambridge UP, 2002.

Hennegan, Alison. 'Aerobatics.' Rev. of *Staring at the Sun. New Statesman* 3 October 1986: 38–9.

Herbert, Susannah. 'Julian Barnes—Not Dead Yet, Just Dying.' *The Sunday Times* 16 March 2008. http://entertainment.timesonline.co.uk/tol/arts_and_entertainment/4/6/2008.

Higdon, David Leon. '"Unconfessed Confessions": The Narrators of Graham Swift and Julian Barnes.' *The British and Irish Novel since 1960.* London: Macmillan, 1991. 174–91.

Hornby, Nick. *Fever Pitch.* London: Victor Gollancz, 1992.

——. 'Much Matter, Few Words.' Rev. of *The Porcupine. Sunday Times* 8 November 1992: Section 6, 11.

Horne, Donald. *The Great Museum: The Re-presentation of History.* London: Pluto, 1984.

Howard, Maureen. 'Fiction in Review.' Rev. of *The Porcupine. Yale Review* 81.2 (1993): 134–9.

Howard, Philip. 'Chattering Hearts in the Quagmire of Love.' Rev. of *Talking It Over*. *Times* 11 July 1991: 16.

Hulbert, Ann. 'The Meaning of Meaning.' Rev. of *Staring at the Sun*. *New Republic* 11 May 1987: 37–9.

Humphreys, Josephine. 'He Gave up Smoking and Irony.' Rev. of *Talking It Over*. *New York Times* 13 October 1991. http://www.nytimes.com/books/01/02/25/Specials/barnes-talking.html/1/22/2005.

Hutcheon, Linda. *A Poetics of Postmodernism: History, Theory, Fiction*. London: Routledge, 1988.

——. *Narcissistic Narrative: The Metafictional Paradox*. Waterloo: Wilfred Laurier UP, 1980.

——. *The Politics of Postmodernism*. New Accents. London: Routledge, 1989.

Imlah, Mick. 'Talking It Over.' Rev. of *Talking It Over*. *TLS* 12 July 1991: 19.

James, Henry. 'The Art of Fiction.' In *Theory of Fiction*. Ed. James E. Miller, Jr. Lincoln: University of Nebraska Press, 1972.

James, P. D. 'Ideal Holmes Exhibition.' Rev. of *Arthur & George Times* 9 July 2005: Books 7.

Jameson, Fredric. *Postmodernism, or, the Cultural Logic of Late Capitalism*. Durham: Duke UP, 1991.

Jeffries, Stuart. 'It's for Self-protection.' Rev. of *Arthur & George*. *Guardian* 6 July 2005. http://www.guardian.co.uk/print0,3858,5232062-103680,00.html/9/3/2005.

'Jeanette Winterson 1959– '. http://www.enotes.com/contemporary-literary-criticism/winterson-j/4/6/2008.

Jones, Lewis. 'Botching the Detectives.' Rev. of *Arthur & George*. *Telegraph* 4 July 2005. http://www.telegraph.co.uk/core/Content/displayPrintable.jhtml?xml=/arts/2005/07/03bob . . . /9/3/2005.

Jordanova, Ludmilla. *History in Practice*. London: Arnold, 2000.

Joseph-Vilain, Mélanie. 'The Writer's Voice(s) in *Flaubert's Parrot*.' *Q/W/E/R/T/Y* 11 (2001): 183–8.

Kakutani, Michiko. 'Books of the Times.' Rev. of *Before She Met Me*. *New York Times* 17 December 1986: C26.

——. '"Love, Etc.": An Old Love Triangle Reassembled in a New Decade.' *The New York Times* 9 February 2001. http://www.nytimes.com/2001/02/09/arts/09BOOK.html?ex=1106542800&en=6a3ac746e . . . /1/22/2005.

Kastor, Elizabeth. 'Julian Barnes' Big Questions.' *Washington Press Book World* 18 May 1987: 9.

Kemp, Peter. 'Conan Doyle to the Rescue.' Rev. of *Arthur & George*. *The Sunday Times* 26 June 2005: 37–8.

Kempton, Adrian. 'A Barnes Eye View of France.' Rev. of *Cross Channel*. *Franco-British Studies* 22 (1996): 92–101.

Kermode, Frank. 'Obsessed with Obsession.' Rev. of *Flaubert's Parrot*. *New York Review of Books* 25 April 1985: 15–16.

——. 'Stowaway Woodworm.' Rev. of *A History of the World in 10¹/₂ Chapters*. *London Review of Books* 22 June 1989: 20.

Korte, Barbara. 'Julian Barnes's *England, England*: Tourism as a Critique of Postmodernism.' In *The Making of Modern Tourism: The Cultural History of the British Experience, 1600–2000*. Ed. Harmut Berghoff, Barbara Korte, Ralf Schneider and Christopher Harvie. Basingstoke: Palgrave, 2002. 285–303.

Kotte, Christina. *Ethical Dimensions in British Historiographic Metafiction: Julian Barnes, Graham Swift, Penelope Lively*. Trier: WVT Wissenschaftlicher Verlag Trier, 2001.

Kotte, Claudia. 'Random Patterns? Orderly Disorder in Julian Barnes's *A History of the World in 10¹/₂ Chapters*.' *Arbeiten aus Anglistik und Amerikanistik* 22 (1997): 107–28.

Krasteva, Yonka. 'Julian Barnes's *The Porcupine*: Recent Balkan History under Western Eyes.' *Zeitschrift fur Anglist und Amerikanistik* 48.4 (2000): 343–53.

Krist, Gary. 'She Oughtn't to Have Been in Pictures.' Rev. of *Before She Met Me*. *New York Times* 28 December 1986. http://www.nytimes.com/books/01/02/25/specials/Barnes-before.html/1/22/2005.

LaCapra, Dominick. *History & Criticism*. Ithaca: Cornell UP, 1985.

Lanchester, John. 'A Vision of England.' *Daily Telegraph* [London] 29 August 1998: A5.

Larkin, Philip. *The Less Deceived*. London: Marvell Press, 1955.

Lawson, Mark. 'A Short History of Julian Barnes.' *Independent Magazine* 13 July 1991: 34–6.

——. 'The Gender Bender Gets It Wrong.' Rev. of *Staring at the Sun*. *Sunday Times* 28 September 1986: 53.

Lázaro, Alberto. 'The Techniques of Committed Fiction: In Defence of Julian Barnes's *The Porcupine*.' *Atlantis* 22.1 (2000): 121–31.

Lee, Alison. *Realism and Power: Postmodern British Fiction*. London: Routledge, 1990.

Leith, William. 'Where Nothing Really Happens.' *Independent on Sunday* 2 May 1993: 13–14.

Levin, Bernard. 'Metroland: Thanks for the Memories.' Rev. of *Metroland*. *The Sunday Times* 6 April 1980: 42.

Lewis, Georgie. 'Julian and Arthur and George'. http://www.powells.com/authors/barnes.html/5/17/2007.

Lodge, David. 'The Home Front.' Rev. of *Staring at the Sun*. *New York Review of Books* 7 May 1987: 21.

――. 'The Novel Now: Theories and Practices.' *Novel: A Forum on Fiction* 21.2–3 (1988): 125–38.

Lyotard, Jean-François. *The Postmodern Condition: A Report on Knowledge*, In Theory and History of Literature, Volume 10. Trans. Geoff Bennington and Brian Massumi. Minneapolis: University of Minnesota Press, 1984.

MacCannell, Dean. *The Tourist: A New Theory of the Leisure Class.* New York: Schocken, 1976.

McCloskey, James. 'Julian Barnes in Conversation with James McCloskey.' *The Brooklyn Rail* September 2005. http://www.thebrooklynrail.org/books/sept05/barnes.html/ 5/13/2007.

McGrath, Patrick. 'Julian Barnes.' *Bomb* 21 (1987): 20–3.

McGraw, Erin. 'Roshomon in Love, 10 Years Later.' Rev of *Love, etc. San Francisco Chronicle* 11 February 2001. http://www.sfgate.com/cgi-bin/article.cgi?file=/chronicle/archive/2001/02/11/RV103407 . . . /4/24/2006.

McHale, Brian. *Postmodernist Fiction.* London: Methuen, 1987.

Mellors, John. 'Authorized Versions.' Rev. of *Flaubert's Parrot. London Magazine* October 1984: 82–3.

――. 'Bull's Blood.' Rev. of *Before She Met Me. London Magazine* April–May 1982: 133–4.

Millington, Mark I. and Alison S. Sinclair. 'The Honourable Cuckold: Models of Masculine Defence.' *Comparative Literature Studies* 29.1 (1992): 1–19.

Miracky, James J. 'Replicating a Dinosaur: Authenticity Run Amock in the "Theme Parking" of Michael Crichton's *Jurassic Park* and Julian Barnes's *England, England*'. *Critique: Studies in Contemporary Fiction* 45.2 (2004): 163–9. http://find/galegroup.com.ezproxy.lakeheadu.ca/itx/printdoc.do?&pr . . . /6/29/2007.

Montrose, Louis. 'Professing the Renaissance: The Poetics and Politics of Culture.' In *The New Historicism.* Ed. H. Aram Veeser. New York: Routledge, 1989. 15–36.

Moore, Caroline. 'A Far from Elementary Novel.' Rev. of *Arthur & George. Sunday Telegraph* 4 July 2005. http://www.telegraph.co.uk/core/Content/displayPrintable.jhtml?xml=/arts/2005/07/03/bob.

――. 'How to Pass the Acid Test.' Rev. of *The Lemon Table. Sunday Telegraph* 7 March 2004. http://web.lexis-nexis.com/universe/document?_m=7a7ebbc11f18d8a812be5ca92 . . . /8/4/2005.

Moseley, Merritt. *Understanding Julian Barnes.* Columbia: University of South Carolina Press, 1997.

Nicholl, Charles. 'Oliver's Riffs.' Rev. of *Talking It Over. London Review of Books* 25 July 1991: 19.

Nünning, Vera. 'The Invention of Cultural Traditions: The Construction and Deconstruction of Englishness and Authenticity in Julian Barnes's *England, England*'. *Anglia* 119 (2001): 58–76. http://julianbarnes.com/docs/nunning.pdf.

Oates, Joyce Carol. 'But Noah Was Not a Nice Man.' Rev. of *A History of the World in 10½ Chapters*. *New York Times* 1 October 1989. http://www.nytimes.com/books/01/02/25/specials/barnes-history.html/1/22/2005.

O'Hagan, Simon. 'The Game's Afoot! It Could Be a Case for Sherlock Holmes.' Rev. of *Arthur & George*. *Independent* 2 September 2005. http://enjoyment.independent.Co.uk/books/reviews/articles296511.ece/9/2/2005.

O'Regan, Nadine. 'Cool, Clean Man of Letters.' *The Sunday Business Post* 29 June 2003. http://archives.tcm.ie/businesspost/2003/06/29/story38220037.asp.

Parini, Jay. 'Two Clever Lads from London.' Rev. of *Metroland*. *New York Times* 3 May 1987. http://www.nytimes.com/books/01/02/25/specials/barnes-metro.html/1/22/2005.

Parrinder, Patrick. 'Sausages and Higher Things.' Rev. of *The Porcupine*. *London Review of Books* 11 February 1993: 18–19.

Pateman, Matthew. 'Is There a Novel in this Text? Identities of Narrative in *Flaubert's Parrot*.' In *L' Exil et l' Allégorie dans le Roman Anglophone Contemporain*. Ed. Michel Morel. Paris: Editions Messene, 1998. 37–47.

——. *Julian Barnes*. Writers and Their Work Series. Horndon: Northcote, 2002.

——. 'Julian Barnes and the Popularity of Ethics.' In *Postmodern Surroundings*. Postmodern Studies Series. Volume 9. Ed. Steven Earnshaw. Amsterdam: Rodopi, 1994. 179–91.

Paulin, Tom. 'National Myths.' Rev. of *Metroland*. *Encounter* June 1980: 63.

Pease, Donald. 'Author.' In *Critical Terms for Literary Study*. Ed. Frank Lentricchia and Thomas McLaughlin. Chicago: University of Chicago Press, 1990. 105–17.

Puddington, Arch. 'After the Fall.' Rev. of *The Porcupine*. *Commentary* 95.5 (1993): 62–4.

Quinn, Anthony. 'The Ship of State.' Rev. of *A History of the World in 10½ Chapters*. *New Statesman and Society* 28 June 1989: 38.

Rafferty. Terence. 'Watching the Detectives.' Rev. of *Flaubert's Parrot*. *Nation* 6/13 July 1985: 21–2.

Robinson, David. 'Ideal Holmes Exhibition.' Rev. of *Arthur & George*. *The Scotsman* 2 July 2005. http://news.scotsman.com/print.cfm?id=726232005/9/2/2005.

Rubinson, Gregory. *The Fiction of Rushdie, Barnes, Winterson and Carter: Breaking Cultural and Literary Boundaries in the Work of Four Postmodernists.* Jefferson, N.C. and London: McFarland, 2005.

Rumbold, Judy. 'What Jamie Could Teach Julian.' Rev. of *The Pedant in the Kitchen. Guardian* 15 October 2003. http://www.guardian.co.uk/g2/story/ 0,3604,1062990,00.html/6/9/2006.

Rusbridger, Alan. 'All about My Father.' *Guardian* 8 May 2000. http://books. guardian.co.uk/departments/generalfiction/story/0,21 . . . /4/5/2008.

Said, Edward. *Orientalism.* New York: Vintage-Random House, 1978.

Sansom, Ian. 'Half-Timbering, Homosexuality, and Whingeing.' Rev. of *England, England. London Review of Books* 1 October 1998: 31–2.

Scammell, Michael. 'Trial and Error.' Rev. of *The Porcupine. The New Republic* 4 January 1993. http://proquest.umi.com/pqdweb?index=0&did= 5151621&SrchMode=1&sid=1&Fmt=3& . . . /7/14/2006.

Scott, James. 'Parrot as Paradigm: Infinite Deferral of Meaning in *Flaubert's Parrot.' Ariel* 21.3 (1990): 57–68.

Sesto, Bruce. *Language, History, and Metanarrative in the Fiction of Julian Barnes.* Studies in Twentieth-Century Brit. Lit. Series. Volume 3. New York: Peter Lang, 2001.

Shakespeare, William. *King Henry IV, Part I.* Arden Shakespeare Paperbacks. Ed. A. R Humphreys. London: Methuen, 1966.

——. 'Sonnet 116.' The Sonnets *and* A Lover's Complaint. Ed. John Kerrigan. London: Penguin, 1986. 134.

Showalter, Elaine. 'Careless Talk Costs Wives.' Rev of *Love, etc. The Guardian* 5 August. http://books.guardian.co.uk/reviews/generalfiction/ 0,350405,00.html /4/24/2006.

Shrimpton, Nicholas. 'Bourgeois v Bohemian.' *New Statesman* 28 March 1980: 483.

Smith, Amanda. 'Julian Barnes.' *Publisher's Weekly* 3 November 1989: 73–4.

Spurling, Hilary. 'In Full Feather.' Rev. of *Something to Declare. Daily Telegraph* 19 January 2002: A3.

Stevenson, Randall. *The Last of England?* Oxford English Lit. History Series. Volume 12. Oxford: Oxford UP, 2004.

Stone, Robert. 'The Cold Peace.' Rev. of *The Porcupine. New York Times* 13 December 1992. http://www.nytimes.com/books/01/02/25/specials/ barnes-porcupine. Html/1/22/2005.

Stout, Mira. 'Chameleon Novelist.' *New York Times Magazine* 22 November 1992. http://www.nytimes.com/books/01/02/25/specials/ barnes-chameleon.html/ 1/22/2005.

Sturgess, Philip. 'Metroland.' Rev. of *Metroland. The Literary Review* 16–19 May 1980: 10.

Summerscale, Kate. 'Julian Barnes: Life as he Knows It.' http://www.
telegraph.co.uk/Core/Content/displayPrintable.jhtml;jses . . . /4/6/2008.

Swanson, Carl. 'Old Fartery and Literary Dish.' *Salon Magazine* 13 May 1996
http://archive.salon.com/weekly/interview960513.html/5/13/2007.

Swift, Graham. *Ever After*. 1992. New York: Vintage, 1993.

Tait, Theo. 'Twinkly.' Rev. of *Arthur & George*. *London Review of Books*
1 September 2005: 25–6.

Tayler, Christopher. 'Like Choosing between Bacon and Egg and Bacon and
Tomato.' Rev. of *The Lemon Table*. *London Review of Books* 15 April 2004:
17–18.

Taylor, D. J. 'A Newfangled and Funny Romp.' Rev. of *A History of the World
in 10½ Chapters*. *Spectator* 24 June 1989: 40.

——. 'Fearful Symmetry.' Rev of *Talking It Over*. *New Statesman & Society* 19
July 1991: 35.

Tew, Philip. *The Contemporary British Novel*. London: Continuum, 2004.

Theroux, Alexander. 'Was It Something They Said?' Rev. of *Talking It Over*.
Washington Post Book World 13 October 1991: 5.

Thorpe, Vanessa. 'Mystery Man.' *Observer* 14 August 2005. http://books.
guardian.co.Uk/bookerprize2005/story/0,1549463,00.html/4/5/2008.

Thwaite, Anthony. 'A Course in Creativity.' Rev. of *Before She Met Me*.
Observer 18 April 1982: 31.

Todd, Richard. *Consuming Fictions: The Booker Prize and Fiction in Britain Today*.
London: Bloomsbury, 1996.

Updike, John. 'A Pair of Parrots.' Rev. of *Flaubert's Parrot*. *The New Yorker* 22
July 1985: 86–7.

Vianu, Lidia. 'Giving up Criticism is Much Easier than Giving up Alcohol
or Tobacco.' *România Literara* 13–19 December 2000. http://lidiavianu.
scriptmania.com/julian_barnes.htm/13/5/2007.

Walter, Natasha. 'Our Mutual Friends.' Rev. of *Arthur & George*. *The Guardian*
2 July 2005: 26.

Waugh, Harriet. 'Green-eyed.' Rev. of *Before She Met Me*. *Spectator* 17 April
1982: 22.

Waugh, Patricia. *Practising Postmodernism, Reading Modernism*. London:
Routledge, 1989.

Webb, Alex. 'Barnes and France: Love Requited.' *BBC News* 18 January 2002.
http://news.bbc.co.uk/1/entertainment/arts/1766800.stm/6/6/2005.

White, Hayden. 'The Value of Narrativity in the Representation of Reality.'
Critical Inquiry 7 (1980): 5–27.

——. *Tropics of Discourse: Essays in Cultural Criticism*. Baltimore: Johns
Hopkins UP, 1978.

Wiegand, David. 'England Imagined as a Theme Park in Julian Barnes's
Witty Satire.' Rev. of *England, England*. *San Francisco Chronicle* 23 May 1999.

http://www.sfgate.com/cgibin/article.cgi?file=/chronicle/archive/1999/05/23/RV89562.DTL/11/9/2005.

Williams, David. 'Paperbacks of the Month: Fiction.' Rev. of *Metroland*. *Times* 1 August 1981: 9.

Wood, Michael. 'In Search of Love and Judgement.' Rev. of *A History of the World in 10¹/₂ Chapters*. *TLS* 30 June–6 July 1989: 713.

Wroe, Nicholas. 'Literature's Mister Cool.' *Guardian* 29 July 2000. http://books.Guardian.co.uk/departments/generalfiction/story/0,34 . . . /4/5/2008.

'You Ask the Questions: Julian Barnes.' *Independent* 16 January 2002. http://enjoyment.Independent.co.uk/books/interviews/story.jsp?story=114605/6/6/2005.

INDEX